CHASING
EDEN

CHASING
EDEN

Design Inspiration from the Gardens at
HORTULUS FARM

JACK STAUB & RENNY REYNOLDS
photographs by ROB CARDILLO

Timber Press
PORTLAND, OREGON

Published in 2020 by Timber Press, Inc.
The Haseltine Building
133 S.W. Second Avenue, Suite 450
Portland, Oregon 97204-3527
timberpress.com

Printed in China
Text and cover design by Stacy Wakefield Forte

ISBN 978-1-60469-873-2

Catalog records for this book are available from the
Library of Congress and the British Library.

THIS BOOK IS DEDICATED
TO OUR LONGTIME FARM
MANAGER BOB RITCHIE
AND HIS WIFE, ROSE,
WITHOUT WHOSE TIRELESS
DEVOTION, FRIENDSHIP,
AND HARD WORK, WE SIMPLY
WOULD NOT EXIST.

~~

CONTENTS

~~

In their hearts, all
gardeners are in
pursuit of "Eden"—
or their own very
personal vision of it.
An earthly paradise
of visual beauty and
emotional solace.

*Our charge has been to deformalize
classical conceits—as in the Birch
Walk, which takes the classic formal
allée idea and loosens it with great
drifts of hostas and ferns.*

A place in which the mind can rest and the soul be renewed.
A place that embraces all God's children and reconnects us with
something greater than ourselves. We started with an essentially
garden-less if historic 15-acre farmstead on a creek in rural
Pennsylvania and, over the past 40 years, have employed the elements
of classical garden design to transform its unruly topography into
our vision of an earthly paradise. One of the chief lessons we have
learned is that classic garden tenets, while not meant to be broken
exactly, can surely be bent to suit your particular site and situation.
Therefore, in each chapter of this book, we will discuss one or more
elements of classical garden theory and then walk you through
how we have sought to apply them to a less-than-optimal setting,
although one with its own very strong sense of place. To us, that's
the wondrous thing: once you've armed yourself with the correct
theoretical knowledge, you'll be amazed at how malleable and
adaptable it can be. As well, each chapter will include a sidebar
detailing the history of classical garden theory, with all its fascinating
fads, feuds, and ultimate cohesion, a second sidebar highlighting a
particular notion introduced in that chapter, and, finally, a list of "dos"
and "don'ts" related to the theory or theories in question. We regard
all these as being applicable to a property of any size or description
and of interest to a gardener of any degree of experience.

Renny often tells the story of the day he closed on our farm.
The couple who sold the property to us had lived in our stone house
but rented out the barns to other individuals, who used them for
storage and boarded horses; although, from the state of the barns
and stalls and the number of rust-pocked vehicles that littered the
upper drive when we first arrived, any horse with any horse sense
would have taken one look and cantered off in some other direction.
But Renny, truly needing a pastoral break from the nightly events
he was staging at the legendary Studio 54 in New York (yes, he put
Bianca Jagger on that white horse . . .) and having been enamored
of horticulture from an early age, had fallen in love with the farm,
literally at a single, heart-stopping glance, as his realtor plunged him
into our secret little valley for the first time. And so, completely
undeterred, he handed the most sizeable check he had ever
written, thanks to the success of Studio 54, over to the local notary,

*Our hope is that the
gardens that surround
the stone house are
sufficiently spontaneous
and informally sited
to suit the truly rural
nature of our place
on earth.*

whereupon the husband of the couple in question tossed the house keys across the conference room table and announced: "Good luck keeping that place up!"

Let's get one thing clear upfront: we arrived on the farm with our own very individual expertises. So, while I, Jack, am mainly a writer and may be setting our story and gardening philosophy down in these pages, if you must honor someone for what has been accomplished at Hortulus Farm, you must immediately swivel your attention to my partner of the last 40 years. Aside from his amazing ability to conceive event design on a huge scale, Renny has a degree in landscape architecture and urban planning from the University of Wisconsin, and it is his eye and talent alone that saw possibility where I, at least in the beginning, saw only what was baldly staring back at me, and it is his vision that has made our gardens what they are today. If you have the pleasure of meeting him, do tell him you admire what he imagined out of a complex rural perplexity. I promise you: he will bask in it. And deserves it. And I will admire you for it.

When we arrived on the farm in 1979, it was right on the edge of dereliction. The stone foundations of the two immense dairy barns were crumbling, and most of the stalls were filled with piles of rural detritus. Their second-floor floorboards were so rotted through, they were virtually untraversable, and a good third of their siding needed to be replaced. The carriage house, corncrib, and miniature milk barn by the curve in the driveway, charming, vaguely Victorian structures, were superfluous to the previous owners and were therefore, if anything, in an even worse state of repair. In terms of the 18th-century stone house, the electrical and plumbing were scarily antiquated, these functional considerations vying with decorative decisions of an equally terrifying personality for predominance. As a result, in the first year, while creating a garden was certainly on Renny's mind, a lot of the work we did was structural: shoring up and cleaning out the barns, repairing the other outbuildings, and redoing the plumbing and electrical in the house, stripping its original paneling, replastering, and repainting.

Were we incredibly foolish to assume such an undertaking?

We planted this dawn redwood as a puny specimen nearly 40 years ago between the milk pond and the drive, and it's now the tallest thing on the farm.

Undoubtedly, keeping in mind that we were both working full-time in New York and were looking upon this exercise as a destressing weekend idea. But, in the same breath, we were ridiculously optimistic and, reeking with a nearly unassailable combination of positivity and cluelessness, we hired a part-time caretaker to live in the mother-in-law house on the property and keep an eye on things for us during the week in exchange for free rent. And hoped for the best. However, there was one undeniable thing that seemed to override every other consideration or emotion: that kind of lump-in-your-throat feeling that would completely consume us as, every Friday evening, we turned into that long, winding drive, plunged into what was now *our* secret little valley, and saw this sad, magical, dejected place displayed before us. The creek and waterfall cascading through. The classic 18th-century stone farmhouse. The stately barns. The splendid isolation.

And we soon came to understand that time would, in the end, be our staunchest ally. That we were in it for the long haul. We had just become stewards of a piece of genuine Americana, however down-at-the-heels. And, honestly, we also came to understand that there could be beauty in such decline, for its being such a poor farm meant that no one had made unsympathetic modern improvements or additions to any of the buildings. Every piece of architecture remained purely what it was—what it had always been—and it was our job as stewards of such a place to guard and enhance its uncannily pristine persona. And that was an idea that would always temper and inform our decisions, especially the ones plucked from and influenced by the classic garden vernacular, as we began to make a garden.

Vista. Axis. Enclosure. Reveal. Surprise. Focal points. Plant palette. Water features. Hardscape. Garden appointments. All these classical ideals would, in the end, be filtered through the lens of our own very strong, very particular sense of place. And so, with just the smallest twinge of trepidation, we began chasing our Eden: the creation of a classically conceived but, also, profoundly personal vision of an American farm garden—a goal we continue to pursue to this day.

ORIENTATION

efore we get too much further,
we think it would be sensible for
us to briefly orient you to the various
gardens we have created on the farm
in the past 40 years, numbering almost
two dozen in all. To that end, we're
going to take you on a verbal tour
following the route we take when we
tour garden groups around the farm.
We're going to number, capitalize,
and italicize each garden as we go,
so you can understand what is what.
So: we start at the nursery, at the
southern perimeter of the property
on Thompson Mill Road, pointing
out, to the right, *1. The Peony Ribbon*
extending sinuously east toward our
driveway, then traveling north down *2.
The Birch Walk* to enter *3. The Woodland
Walk* to the west as we reach the
lake. We travel west along the south
side of the lake to encounter *4. The
Bluebell Lake* up on the left, descend
to Fire Creek, cross a twig bridge, and
continue east on the north side of the
lake to reach *5. The Yellow & Variegated
Foliage Garden*. We then encounter,
on the north side of the walk, *6. The
Topiary Garden*, before climbing up
into *7. The Dell*. From there it's another
climb upslope to the east to the heart
of the farm and *8. The French Garden*, *9.
The Cutting Round*, and *10. The Kitchen
Garden*, followed by *11. The Herb
Gardens*, *12. The Edible Rooms*, and *13.
The Fruit Border* by the chicken house.
Continuing east, we stroll down *14.
The Perennial Borders* to *15. The Pool*

✠ *This little antique putti on a pedestal
invites visitors to Hortulus Farm to descend
to Fire Creek and cross the twig bridge.*

Garden, investigate *16. The Specimen
Arboretum* in back of the pool, then
travel north between *17. The Summer
Borders*, to the Temple Canum, then
up *18. The Pine & Dogwood Allée* to *19.
The Urn Garden* at the top. We then
descend again through *20. The Lajeski
Meadow* to *21. The Mediterranean Garden*,
then back to the Temple Canum via
a lane of goldenrain trees. Finally, we
backtrack down the Perennial Borders,
ending at *22. The Terrace Garden* below
the house, overlooking Fire Creek. It's
a good walk, FYI. We hope that makes
everything perfectly clear. If not, see
the map on the overleaf!

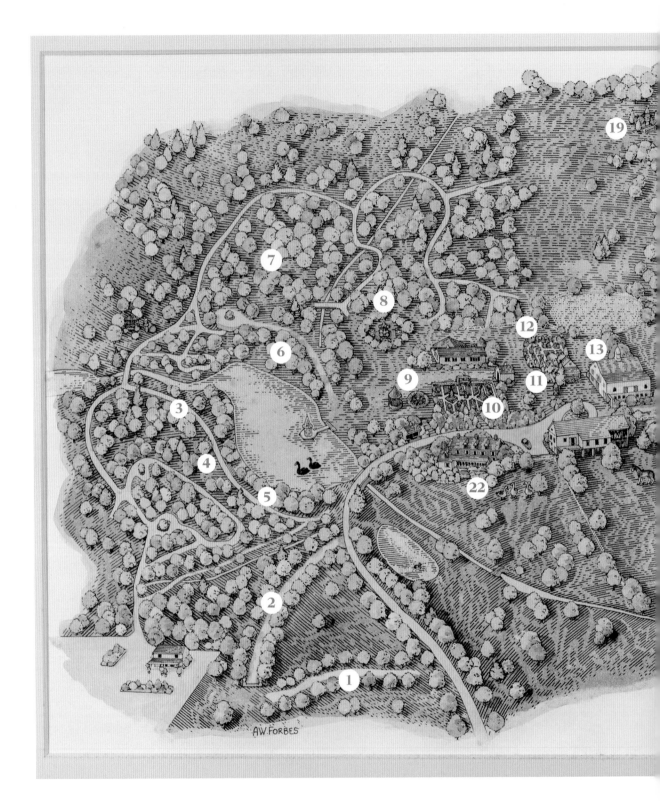

A.W. FORBES

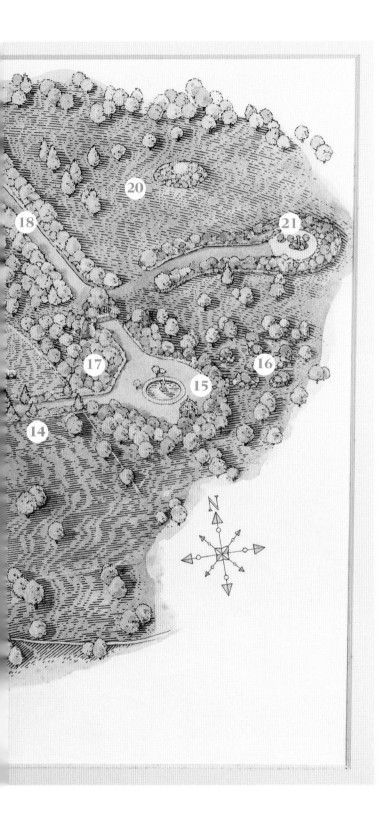

HORTULUS
FARM

On the 31st of January 1728/9 a Deed
was given by Abraham Chapman
to Joseph Warner for 150 acres of Land
in Wrightstown, the bounds of which
were

S 31° W	232	Perches
S W	90	Perches
N 21° E	244	Perches
S E	136	Perches

The same being part of 492 acres which
was granted unto Abraham Chapman
by Benjamin Clark, the same being a part
also of 1000 acres, which whas granted by a
Deed of Lease and Release, dated the
20th and 21st of June, 1683, from William
and John Tanner of London, made to the
said Tanners by Wm Penn, in 1681. —

The consideration paid by Joseph Warner
for the said 150 acres was Ninety seven
Pounds and ten shillings — equal to $253.3.
of our money of the present day

In 1681 William Penn granted unto William
and John Tanner, of London 1000 acres of Land
in Wrightstown — and from a Deed of Lease and
Release of 20th and 21st of June 1683 — unto Benja
Clark, 492 acres of the same — who conveyed

1

The Lay
of the Land

A deed of 1729 detailing the transfer of the farm from William Penn to the Tanner brothers, Benjamin Clark, Abraham Chapman and, ultimately, the Warner family.

We arrived at Hortulus Farm in the fall of 1979, but its story really begins in the year 1681, when the British Quaker William Penn granted 1,000 acres in the soon-to-be county of Bucks, part of the astonishing 45,000 square miles of land he had been deeded by his king, to brothers William and John Tanner of London. A bird flying over Bucks County in those days would have seen dense forest broken with stony outcroppings hugging the silver ribbon of the River de la Ware to the east, with smaller tributaries etching their way through gently undulating woodland giving over to steeper rises as one moved west. But as the mainly English and German immigrants (many of whom were Quakers seeking to escape religious persecution in Europe) arrived to seek their fortunes and

An 1857 survey map
of Wrightstown showing
the considerable holdings
of the Warner clan.

BELOW LEFT
The last generation of
Warner/Thompson
ladies to occupy the
farm can be glimpsed
on the then-open porch
of the house.

BELOW RIGHT
A 1960s view of the
farm showing the lake
that had ceased to exist
by the time we took
possession.

tame their newly acquired parcels in this nearly virgin wilderness, woods fell to pastures and farmland and the construction of neat stone homes of a typically austere Quaker personality. The Tanner brothers, however, never left England, nor did the next owner Benjamin Clark, and those 1,000 acres, known thereafter as the Clark tract, were sold, divided, inherited, and resold, until finally, in 1748, 300 acres of the original tract became the long-term homestead of the Warner family. It was Isaiah Warner, grandson of John and Elizabeth Dawes Warner (whose marriage had reunited the 300 acres), who built the first section of our house on the banks of Fire Creek in 1793.

In the early 19th century, one of the Warner girls married into another old local family, the Thompsons, and, around 1860, the

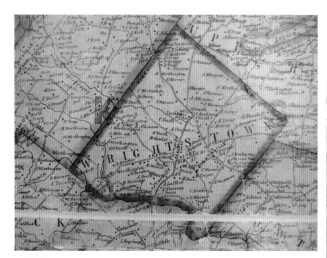

amalgamated Warner/Thompsons went into the dairy business, constructing two immense bank barns in close proximity to the house as well as outbuildings for storing milk, carriages, and equipment, a corncrib to provide winter sustenance for the herds, and a holding pond and stone ice house to keep the canisters of milk cool in summer. And, finally, sometime after the turn of the 20th century, a single-story, shingled mother-in-law house was added on the rise above the stone house. The Warner/Thompsons prospered until 1918 when, after 170 years of tenancy, the last of the family to occupy the farm was compelled to sell the historic homestead to Isaac Ryan, who operated a sawmill on the property. Because of Bucks County's proximity to the Delaware River and the numerous smaller rivers and creeks churning through it, water-powered

A view of the farm taken in the early 20th century, showing the state of near dereliction it was approaching.

BELOW *The lower barn, in which Federal agents discovered a 1,000-gallon still and 20,000 gallons of rye mash in 1932.*

mills were a notable local industry, producing everything from silk to lumber, which could easily be transported up and down the Delaware. We, in fact, reside on Thompson Mill Road, so named because it led from the farm to the grain mill owned by the Thompsons on nearby Neshaminy Creek.

However, in 1931, during both the Great Depression and Prohibition, the collapse of river-based transport tore through the solvency of the district, and Isaac Ryan was forced to close his mill and transfer the farm to a man ostensibly named Benjamin Musselman. Musselman, it transpired, was actually a Philadelphia-based bootlegger named Capriote and, when Federal agents raided the farm in 1932, they discovered 20,000 gallons of rye mash and a 1,000-gallon still in the former dairy barns, making it the largest bootleg bust in Bucks County history. Mr. Capriote posted bond and fled, abandoning the farm, and, by 1933, the property, so derelict it was known locally as "Skunk Hollow," was sold at sheriff's sale for $370.91. There was a notable uptick in the fortunes of the farm from the late 1930s through the early '50s, when it was owned by Colonel Ira and Glenna Fravel, who made some very sympathetic improvements to the house and planted some of the handsome specimen trees we inherited. However, following several more owners, including two women who boarded horses and gave riding lessons in the late 1950s, the farm continued its slow decline and, ultimately reduced to 15 acres, was sold to the key-flinger of Renny's acquaintance sometime in the 1960s.

Enter Us

Renny had been looking for a weekend retreat from New York for a few years and had explored New York state and Connecticut before visiting a friend who had an 18th-century farmstead with a classic stone home just north of us in Carversville, Pennsylvania, in 1977, and it ticked every box on his wish list. Less than an hour and a half from Manhattan. Captivating local vernacular. Antique house. Rural charm. Room for both animals and gardens. He looked at local farms

*As the one and only
Aretha Franklin
postulated, r-e-s-p-e-c-t
is what we have aimed
for in the design of
the gardens.*

throughout Bucks County for almost two years, nearly driving his realtor to the brink of madness until, finally, in 1979, he saw an ad in a local paper for a colonial farmstead in the tiny Central Bucks township of Wrightstown. He immediately contacted his broker and, as they drove down that long, looping driveway for the first time, he fell for the farm at first sight, with the kind of sharp intake of breath that really means business.

I arrived with my burgeoning sack of cluelessness some two months later, but even I knew that, first and foremost, we owed this farm our respect. Our point here is that we weren't some new owners of some recently completed home on a flag lot off some Elm Street somewhere. We had managed to latch onto something, however neglected and mired in disrepair, far more compelling: a 300-year-old legacy of people who had carved that place out of a wilderness, built this little village of pure American architecture there, lived out lives of intense struggle and hopefulness, persevered, prospered and, equally, knew both tears and travails, with our lives and aspirations now tagged onto the end of theirs like the last ribbon on the tail of a kite. And we owed them our respect as well. So, in those first years, we waded in slowly, not wanting to disturb or, worse, damage the bucolic if somewhat melancholic piece of American history that was now, by some wonderful turn of fate, ours. The first obvious and positive idea we did identify was to try and reassemble as much of the original farm acreage as possible and, in the first ten years of our tenancy, we managed to acquire three more adjacent parcels of dwelling-less meadow and woodland of about 30 acres each. This enlarged our original 15 acres considerably so, by 1989, we were the proud owners of a 100-acre, hardscrabble if historic former dairy farm sequestered in a steep valley on a creek in rural Pennsylvania. And, as we have said, no gardens at all.

What we did seem to possess were massive tangles of thorny, vining invasives blanketing the woodlands and roiling through the meadows. During the tenure of the previous owners as well as the owners of the adjacent parcels, wherever lawn gave way to what had been pasture or woodland, Mother Nature had mustered her forces, pervading nearly every square inch with a thicket of saplings, grapevine, poison ivy, bittersweet, and multiflora rose so dense, it was practically impossible to push through without a machete in hand. To say that we spent the first few years of gardening clearing would be an immense understatement. We would arrive on Friday nights and, every Saturday morning, clad in our most impenetrable jeans, long-sleeved shirts, boots, and garden gloves, and armed with chainsaw, shovels, and, yes, machetes, begin to hack back the encroaching tangle. We spent vacations and holidays doing much the same. And, as anyone who has dealt with these invasive monsters can attest, hacking back is only the beginning of this particular enterprise, because these brutes, particularly the nefariously prickly multiflora rose, have, as many have exclaimed, "roots in hell" and, unless they are eradicated, will resprout with even greater tenacity.

In the end, post-clearing, what was revealed to us in terms of an extant garden was not much. There was the Fravel bequest of specimen trees, most notably the magnificent Japanese maple and tulip magnolia on the back lawn, as well as the venerable Kentucky coffee tree, which is perhaps 200 years old, by the lower barn. Other

TOP *An aerial view of the farm sometime in the early '80s, when we had fixed up the outbuildings, constructed the Kitchen Garden fence, and instituted the Perennial Borders.*

RIGHT *British gardening legend Rosemary Verey, here visiting with Jack in the Edible Rooms, is one of the many gardening friends who have helped us on our horticultural journey.*

than that, "we" identified scores of black walnuts, ash, and elms. Seas of buttercups and lesser celandine. Native dogwoods flitting like ghosts through the spring woodland. The rank of immense boxwoods separating house from drive and the big brow of vinca and forsythia across the way. A scattering of spring bulbs. This was both somewhat of a disappointment and a joy as it allowed us (Renny) to do the imagining. We would make a garden there, and it would be ours.

Classical Concerns

On the positive side, what we also had was the substantial ballast of the buildings at the heart of the farm: the stone house, the dairy barns, the milk barn, the carriage shed, the corncrib, and the mother-in-law house on the rise. And, honestly, this is where all gardens need to start: with the architecture of the existing house and other structures, should there be some; in other words (often attributed to Gertrude Jekyll), the garden should curtsy to the house. In effect, gardens radiate from the house, the classical ideal being that the gardens immediately surrounding the house mirror its architecture to some extent, being more symmetrically "room"-like, with hedging and hardscape and terracing, and then become less formal, moving into a more parkland or meadow or wooded idea as one moves away from the house. This, of course, is a blueprint for a property of some size with no unsightly neighboring ideas close by. On a typical suburban lot, the idea of screening and enclosure for a snug feeling of privacy must necessarily be a primary concern.

So we had plenty of architecture but not really of the garden-esque variety. For instance, far from being blessed with the topographical ideal of a house situated on the highest elevation on the property so that our classically-inspired gardens could be disposed below us, our 1793 house was stubbornly positioned on nearly the lowest point on the farm, on Fire Creek, which runs west to east through the bottom of the property, with the bulk of our acreage rising steeply from the creek bed to the north and south. Our home site was clearly cut into the northern slope of the creek and leveled as, across the equally leveled drive, which runs past the front door, an enormously steep bank rises northward, capped by the mother-in-law house at the summit, continuing thence in the same direction into pasture and woodland. In the classical lexicon, steep slopes like these would generally be solved by the application of terracing, but formal terracing seemed to us totally inappropriate to our American farm vernacular. Then there was the close proximity and total asymmetry of the dairy barns and other outbuildings. In the European vernacular of centuries past, these buildings with the house usually surrounded a courtyard with sympathetic architecture on all sides, creating an orderly and linear whole with just the right amount of cobblestoned charm. Such was not our case. Our barns

Many of our natively rural areas have remained as such and are really the framework for the more formal gestures we have initiated.

are disposed beyond the house around the big loop that crowns the driveway so that, in effect, the black-topped drive is the single, unifying element of the whole architectural arrangement. Not very auspicious.

And what of other classical considerations? What of views, axes, and vistas? Progression? Enclosure and reveal? Focal points? Water features? Beds and borders? Garden rooms? Well, in terms of "rooms," we were, so to speak, still clearly in search of the greater "house." As for vistas and axes, yes, there was the relatively flat viewshed running west to east along the northern side of the creek and out into the former cow pasture between the barns but, in the main, our vistas were of those north and south flanks rising to meet the horizon

TAKE NOTE

Our opinion is, the first thing any gardener needs to do when faced with a new property, especially one of some size and even one as unruly as ours, is absolutely nothing. Like sit-on-your-hands nothing. Well, not quite: we encourage a good bit of investigation and nosing around but, mainly, this is an exercise in mental absorption and note-taking. We can remove from this equation any new home sitting on a totally empty lot in suburbia somewhere as, in that case, what you see is all you're ever going to get. But for any other property, whether you are embraced by raw nature or are in a place that has seen some gardening hand, as winter turns to spring, open your eyes and watch as the snows melt and new life begins to emerge. Some marvelous things will happen, and it will be essential that you take note of them. Literally, buy a notebook and start jotting things down as they begin to unfold. Do your best to identify the surrounding trees and shrubs as they start to green up. Look for the impertinent noses of spring bulbs as they push their way through the previously frozen tundra. If something does develop, draw a diagram of it as to its situation on the property and note bloom time, etc. Then, through the season, continue to take notes and make diagrams of what blooms where and when, also noting

A blackboard at the entrance to Sissinghurst welcomes visitors to share in the daily thoughts and priorities of the gardeners there.

blossom color, random thoughts for companion planting, where hedging or hardscape might create interest or surprise, ideas for focal points or a water feature or a longed-for vegetable patch, etc. Let your eyes and brain do all the heavy lifting that first season. And then, over the following winter, factoring in everything that's appeared and flowered and percolated over that first season, begin to make a plan.

substantially above us. Aside from the architecture, focal points were not even a consideration as we had no real views leading anywhere and, with all that woodland, we had plenty of enclosure, but what was generally revealed was invasive-choked former dairy pasture. And, truthfully, another gnawing consideration was, while we certainly wanted gardens, what we had also fallen in love with was the frankly rural nature and snug feeling of our cloistered little valley with its thick band of forest and farmland protecting us from any other note of civilization.

In the end, for the most part, our woodlands would remain as such, although they were all crying out for some basic forestry maintenance, especially the removal of dead wood and thinning of saplings. Our former farm fields, some on the road let to a local farmer for corn and soy, were up for grabs. So, as we mulled and cleared, identified and shored up and mulled some more, we took at least two years to really plunge into garden making. And when I say "we" at this juncture, let me reiterate what I really mean: I was nearly haplessly following Renny around, season to season, wondering what on earth our next step might be. Renny, on the other hand, like a dog on a scent, nose to air, was, in the fog of my bewilderment, endlessly sniffing out the horticultural possibilities that might lie before us. Ultimately, these would be legion.

Renny, the master of all he surveys, on one of our first work carts with our beloved Casper and Louise.

 In the 1st century AD, Pliny the Younger assigned the virtue of otium to a garden, as in this tranquil moment at the Villa d'Este near Rome, signifying a place of both symmetry and serenity.

Classic Garden
PRINCIPLES

"Classic garden principles," although firmly rooted in most people's minds as being a vaguely British idea, are, in fact, far from being the domain of any particular Euro-culture. As Gertrude Jekyll wrote in *Garden Ornament* (1918), "It is, in fact, almost impossible actually to define a style, for whether a garden is called Italian, French, Dutch, or English, each of these merges into and overlaps the other, for they all have features in common that vary only in detail or treatment." However, England seems to have been the ethnic funnel through which this Continental polyglot of ideas and ideals was channeled to arrive in its current form, although not without its share of warring factions and missteps. England, in fact, prior to the 16th century, had virtually no garden ethos of which to speak. With practically any European nation one could name constantly fortifying itself to overrun and overtake another, ruling class abodes and their tenancies were, in the main, small fortified cities built at the highest elevations available for defense and, eschewing the horticultural possibilities those vantage points might have offered, looked inward instead into protected courtyards, in which only the most rudimentary plots were given over to the production of food for man and beast. It is actually in 1st-century Italy that the seed of what we now understand as classic garden principles was planted, Pliny the Younger assigning in that period the virtue of *otium* to the garden, this translating to a place of calm, serenity, and renewal, further describing a restful place of symmetrically disposed planting beds and water features, providing soothing sensory delight, and strolling paths cloistered between tall hedges or linear ranks of trees. "Golden" formulas defining ideal spatial relationships were the rage: length to breadth in terms of a building or garden plot, with hardscape ruling. This pretty order, however, was destined to go to hell in a handcart with the terrible 5th-century retro-slide into the Dark Ages.

DO

Drink in with joy what you own. Everything about it. What was it about that particular house, that particular site, that particular feeling in the pit of your stomach that made this choice the right choice? Work hard to identify the elements and features that made you feel that way, letting possibility guide your thoughts. Then figure out what you can do to enhance that very particular mood and ambience.

Take the time to identify your primary goals. If your goal is an outdoor living space or a pool or a vegetable garden, do some research as to the requirements involved. If there is something unsightly in your viewshed, think about enclosure and screening options. If you are a total horticultural neophyte, buy some books or investigate some online blogs that will give you at least some of the knowledge and tools you will need to proceed.

Make friends with your local nurseries. As they pretty much stock what will work in your zone, not only will you begin to understand what species and cultivars are suitable for your particular situation, but these knowledgeable folks can offer you expert advice on issues ranging from siting and soil quality to the best ideas for sun or shade, wet or dry areas. They will also probably install the big stuff you purchase from them for an additional cost. "Buy local" is a scheme that works for everyone.

Concentrate on hardscape, in the beginning. This can be a messy and plant-wrecking exercise. If your garden needs terracing or retaining walls or sets of steps, or if you are keen for a stone patio or in-ground pool or grape arbor or grotto, that's where you should be headed your first year. Any planting can most happily wait until your hardscape is complete.

Try to wrap your head around the idea of succession planting (i.e., figuring out what blooms early, midseason, and late) in terms of shrubs and perennials, so that your garden will sparkle all season long. In fact, an excellent endeavor, should you encounter a lull in blossom as you begin your planting, is to simply go see what's in bloom at your local nursery, buy some, and pop it in. Bingo!

DON'T

Take on too much too soon: there is no sense in overwhelming yourself. If you have identified a big, primary goal like a stone patio or pool area or vegetable garden, figure out the optimum siting and dimensions for it and wrestle that to the ground first. It will give you a kind of anchor that will inform and direct your auxiliary choices. Does it need hedging or enclosure? A pergola for shade? A pretty border to soften the hard edges? A pair of urns or planters to announce it? One foot in front of the other.

Go crazy with color. A rainbow palette of foliage and blossom will only result in a Disney-esque assault on your senses. Start with a limited palette, just a few colors: a blue/yellow/white theme, a pink/blue/white idea, or all green and white are lovely. To us, reds, oranges, the brightest yellows, and the deepest purples, especially in terms of foliage, are always the trickiest, so, at least in the beginning, restrain yourself.

Go it alone if you are floundering. Nurseries, books, and blogs are all excellent sources of inspiration and information but, sometimes, especially if your property is of some size, getting design help will help stave off "tears before bedtime," as Nanny used to say. Ask around and interview some local landscape architects or designers who strike your fancy (visit some of their projects first, just to make sure), then hire the one who's the best fit to help you make a plan.

Think that anything that's invasive or unruly out there is going to solve itself. If you've got anything like what we inherited, very simply, you've got to deal with it. Dig out the invasives. Eradicate the stubborn viners like grapevine and poison ivy. Bring that sector of your garden under your domain, not theirs. It's the only way to commence gardening in the company of these thugs. Don't hesitate to be brutal.

Despair. All gardeners have doubts, make wrong decisions, face seemingly insurmountable issues, and have plants that refuse to cooperate. Shit happens. Things die. The wonder of a garden is that it is a constantly evolving, living thing. You are on this ride for the long haul. Certainly, there will be a bit of loss and heartbreak. But also the wonders of triumph and deep, abiding satisfaction.

2
—

Long Views
Vista & Axis

†

A long view through the woods at the eastern perimeter of the farm to the neighboring farm and the Windybush Valley.

When, finally, we were able to view our extended acreage without entanglement and had gathered our horticultural wits about us, we began setting our first, extensive, Anglo-ideal in motion: identifying both the long views and the beginnings of the shape of the gardens. What viewsheds did we already possess that might begin to dictate a plan? What sites were ripe for "destination" status, and how would one perceive that one had arrived at such? What focal points might be in the running to herald said arrival? How would the eye be focused and directed, and how would one travel through the gardens? Paths? Steps? Lanes? Bridges? And what of the idea of progression?

Certainly, as our gardens have evolved, one progresses from one moment to another; but, usually, classical progression transitions from formality to informality as one moves farther from the house, and our idea of progression is more in the line of an assemblage of disparate if sympathetic horticultural ideas of varying degrees of formality loosely linked by paths and turf. In actuality, it would be difficult to call any of these various garden moments really formal, an idea that would become a signature of our greater gardens as we continued our horticultural journey.

A good example of this departure from the relative severity of classical garden design is our interpretation of garden "rooms," these generally of a geometric nature (including circular) and achieved by the clever placement of walls or hedging or ranks of trees in the classical vernacular. We suppose you could say our "moments," chanced upon in the woodland and elsewhere, are "room-esque," i.e., all are enclosed by woodland or some form of structure or hedging. To us, these "moments" are really more horticultural gestures or pastiches, based in formal theory but deformalized in terms of how one comes upon them or in the purposeful informality of their siting or planting to better suit our American farm vernacular.

A fall view down the entrance drive to the farm, just before one plunges into the valley.

OPPOSITE *The narrow turf path that runs along the south side of the lake in early spring.*

Always in the back of our minds is that incontrovertible fact: we are not a stately home in England or France or Italy. We are who we are, and taking the classical idea and stripping away its rigidity— through either siting, plant palette, or layout, so that there is an ease and almost a carelessness to the gesture that allows it to coexist sympathetically with native meadow and woodland—has become, in a way, our signature.

One axis and viewshed was glaringly obvious: the narrow flat bit that ran along the creek at the bottom of the property west to east, was broken by the lake, then, rising to the drive, continued to the north of the house, out between the barns and, finally, into newly cleared cow pasture. Ultimately, we decided it made most sense for the long runs to, mainly, run laterally, traveling across the northern and southern slopes, broken occasionally with axes running up- and downslope. While steep, these slopes boasted sufficient undulation to create the occasional near-flat plain running west to east, particularly in the most northeastern corner of the property, which, for the most part, was former dairy pasture and certainly ripe for garden reimagining. As well, alongside the driveway, there was a second clearly leveled lane descending in a dogleg into the valley from a farm shed (now the nursery office) close to the road. We imagined that this might have been the original lane to the house, although this notion still left us more than slightly confounded as most 18th-century houses were built right on the main road as, when they were constructed, the roads were little more than dirt paths running through dense forest or, in the case of a village, from house to house. So, in most of the little 18th-century hamlets that surround us, the houses are clustered in snug proximity, close to both meeting house and tavern, with the farmland surrounding. Our house stands alone on Fire Creek at the end of our very long driveway, nearly a quarter mile from Thompson Mill Road. There is some conjecture that there might have been a road in the 1700s running along the north side of creek, directly opposite the house, but there is no other evidence to support this theory, so the mystery continues. At any rate, that second lane had a definite luster to it as, as one shifted direction at the dogleg, the newly dredged lake and soon-to-be lake pavilion were the visual destinations at the bottom. Axis. Vista. Visual destination. Check.

TOP *The pool plateau is one of the several circular garden constructs dotted around the farm.*

BELOW *The Perennial Borders are part of that long, lateral axis running west to east along Fire Creek, then along the drive north of the house.*

The Birch Walk

Looking down the Birch Walk from the tazza to the lake, just visible through the trees on the left.

By the road, the mystery lane with the dogleg was bordered to the east by a steep bank giving onto planting fields at the top and, to the west, sloped steeply down to a series of runoff streams and wooded flanks. Although partially sapling-ed in, it was easy enough to clear; and, after removing the saplings, plowing, and raking, we seeded it with grass. We then began planting the steep eastern bank with pachysandra to hold it, and, to the west, added a series of hostas to give the path some definition before it fell sharply down to the runoff streams. These hostas now form a thick band on that western perimeter, one type drifting into another, some 40 cultivars in total running the length of the walk. In our always haphazard, transglobal shopping, we discovered a wonderful iron tazza in Italy, rather like an immense champagne glass–shaped urn, and, it, of course, yearning

for a home, was destined to be set as the fulcrum of the dogleg. We plant it seasonally with a colorful selection of perennials and annuals, and it disports itself perfectly as the focal point as one begins one's descent from the farm shed, a distance of about 200 feet. However, the turn of the dogleg was where Renny's imagination took its greatest leap. The lane was straight as a ruler from that point down to the lake, about 300 feet, and, in an ode to landscape architect Fletcher Steele and the gardens he created with Mabel Choate at Naumkeag in Stockbridge, Massachusetts, Renny decreed we would establish a Birch Walk: a turf lane flanked on both sides with ranks of 'Heritage' river birch, a fairly naturalistic gesture although following that classic allée idea—described by ranks of soldier-like trees but, in our "loosening" strategy, underplanted with hostas as well as ostrich and cinnamon ferns, and climaxing in a huge burst of big-leafed petasites as one reached the clearing by the lake.

The purple and white spikes of hosta really do add a refreshing note to this cool, leafy lane.

All our tours start at the nursery and, consequently, the first impression our visitors have of the farm and gardens is the Birch Walk, which is a wonderfully grand tease as one begins to descend, encountering a very rural-feeling wooded lane, the only visual destination being the oddly formal tazza. But then, as one reaches the dogleg and shifts direction, there's an immense feeling of surprise as the Birch Walk is revealed with the unanticipated vista of the lake as the new visual destination at the bottom. And, of course, reversing focus, one looks up from the lake to this steep, green, birch-studded, leafy lane and the focal point of the tazza at the top. The Birch Walk has ultimately proven to be the most enchanting *Midsummer Night's Dream* retreat of cool and shade in the swelter of August: all green and white, the trunks of the birch and their delicate green crowns adding infinite "cool," especially when the hostas are blooming, their white and purple spikes adding still more refreshment. We occasionally feel all we need is Titania wafting through in flowing white with a circlet of lilies of the valley in her hair to complete the pretty picture.

The Italian tazza at the dogleg in the Birch Walk is planted annually with a colorful selection of annuals and perennials.

OPPOSITE *Ostrich ferns prettily unfurling in the Birch Walk.*

The Perennial Borders

As described, our drive ends in a big loop with the lower barn to the right of the loop and the upper barn just beyond the loop to the left, and it was clear that, when the barns were built, some effort had been made to flatten the space extending east between the two. This, again, is essentially an extension of that low-lying west to east axis that is effectively the creek bed skirting around the house to the north, and it is by far the longest, flattest (although still canting north to south to some degree, down to the creek) run we have on the farm, which made it perfect for the classic English borders of our dreams. Renny's vision was that there would be a pair of broad borders flanking an equally broad greensward. So we removed the length of post and rail fence with a central gate linking the corners of the two barns, then ran new post and rail to delineate upper and lower pastures accessed from each of the barns flanking the envisioned borders. Our horses currently occupy the lower pasture and our sheep and goats the upper, so as one tours the farm, wandering out between the borders to the destination of the Pool Garden in the distance with the horses grazing to the right and the sheep and goats to the left, it is, again, that mash-up of "farmness" with classic garden theory that defines Hortulus Farm.

The borders themselves are four rectangular beds, each about 10 feet wide and 100 feet long, two to a side, broken at the midpoint by brief turf lanes leading to big pasture gates. We elected to bend the rule of classical border treatment a bit to better suit our farm vernacular and add a bit of much-needed height in a run that long by placing ranks of cherries and crabapples along its length, a clipped yew hedge to add hard, all-season structure at the back and heighten the sense of enclosure, the occasional shrub, and tall boulevard cypress capping the ends. In the beginning of our tenure on the farm, we grew the four cypresses at the midpoint with the white English climbing roses 'Bobbie James' and 'Wedding Day'. By about ten years in, the cypresses, in effect, had become tuteurs for the roses, which had climbed all the way to their tops, then cascaded down, and the

CLOCKWISE FROM TOP *The crabapples and cherries in the Perennial Borders not only add much-needed height but gorgeous color early in the season.*

Dahlias add a huge amount of late-season punch to the borders.

Our pygmy goats reside in the upper barn and are pastured on the north side of the borders.

Miley in her buttercup-carpeted paddock on the south side of the Perennial Borders.

show when they all bloomed in midsummer was spectacular. Of course, as is the way of all gardens, some attrition is to be expected, and the cypress eventually expired after being strangled by the roses and drowned by a winter and spring of too-soggy feet (we lost half the yew hedges in the same year); they are currently replaced with pencil arborvitae. As noted, although the west to east perennial plane is flattish, it is still a greater part of a north to south slope of sharp incline and, during spring thaw, standing water is our biggest issue. We have tried to solve this problem with the construction of a drainage field above and under the borders, which has alleviated the issue to some extent but, still, in a harsh winter and wet spring, this remains a nagging problem.

The Perennial Borders are planted in a very soft palette of pink, blue, purple, and white.

We never stop trialing new perennials as they come to our attention or replacing plants that have failed to prosper, so long as they fit the soft pink/blue/purple/white palette we chose to favor for this garden. Additionally, aside from the crabs and cherries, we have added the necessary ballast for a run of such a length with an assortment of box balls, spireas, variegated mallows, and other shrubs. This gives the borders the basic groundcover/low-story, mid-story, canopy arrangement that is the classical ideal for the treatment of transitional woodland. The lower and mid-story plantings are extremely broad and inclusive of any perennial we chance upon that fits our pastel palette and will thrive, and we will discuss them at greater length in a subsequent chapter. Our latest fad, fueled by

borders we recently visited in England, has been the addition of dahlias, which—though not strictly perennials but rather tubers to be dug up and replanted annually—supply rousing late-season blossom. That, at their conception and initial implementation, these borders would lead visually to nowhere did absolutely nothing to dissuade Renny from this plan. Needless to say, there was more to follow.

Looking down the Pine & Dogwood Allée to the native dogwood at the center of the Temple Canum and, beyond that, the Pool Garden.

OPPOSITE *One of the native dogwoods we moved from nearby woodland to populate the area around the Temple Canum and the Pine & Dogwood Allée.*

The Pine & Dogwood Allée

The last bit of acreage we acquired in 1989 was essentially the entire northeast corner of the farm, a parcel of about 30 acres. When our neighbor learned we were interested, he opted to double his price, putting it considerably beyond our means. So, fearing something hulking and architecturally suspect or, worse, a whole Toll Brothers complex of the same looming above us, we planted a broad barrier of "screw you" white pines to block whatever might be in our neighboring future. It was at this auspicious moment that our old friend and frequent houseguest Glen Lajeski, a music executive in

*The Pine & Dogwood
Allée leads to the Urn
Garden at the top,
flanked by the partially
wooded Lajeski
Meadow, here shown
in late summer.*

Los Angeles, decided he might like to return to his East Coast roots one day; he not only made an offer on the land, he managed to purchase it for below the original asking price. For years, he gardened and planted parts of this acreage, now preserved in perpetuity, for which we are profoundly grateful. Part of this bequest comprises the Lajeski Meadow, which we have named for Glen because of his constant support and generosity. Now retired, Glen lives on 150 acres in the Sonoma Valley, where he has built a stunning modern house with a jaw-dropping view and a kennel for his show dogs; he grows olives on the bulk of his California estate, supplying us with truly excellent EVOO.

In any case, one week after he acquired the acreage, we hired one of those massive tree spades to move that protective wedge of "screw you" white pines and, one week after that, we had a Pine

& Dogwood Allée: a dramatic new lane about 300 feet long of alternating trees leading straight upslope from the pool plateau at a right angle to the Perennial Borders with the Pool Garden as the fulcrum. Certainly, this is our most extreme case of an axis moving directly upslope vs. across it. The native dogwoods came from the neighboring woods, and we completed this essentially native composition by popping in 'Tardiva' hydrangeas along its length under each dogwood, so that the dogwoods would add blossom interest in spring and the hydrangeas in late summer. Originally, we underplanted both sides with borders of 'Longwood Blue' caryopteris and 'Yellow Gem' potentilla for a very pretty blue and yellow midsummer show but, as the pines and dogwoods matured, they threw the sun-craving caryopteris and potentilla into too much shade, and most of them expired. We've just started replanting the potentilla in a sunnier position along both sides and, just last season, gave this allée some auxiliary punch with the addition of variegated box balls running at intervals on each side along its length. It's become quite a dramatic addition to the garden, not only because of its substantial height and length but because of its unexpectedness as one reaches the Pool Garden and takes a random glance to the left. Of course, in the beginning, it led to nothing but open meadow at the top of the property. Still: vista, axis, reveal, surprise: it's all in a day's work, right?

So, we started making our mark. We had identified some vistas and some axes and made some decisions about the personalities of the gardens that would inhabit those spaces. Still, there was that stubborn sticking point: whatever classical principles we might choose to employ in our garden making would necessarily need to be modified to fit our considerably less than orderly and symmetrical situation. We had one allée with a dogleg, another that led upslope to nowhere except a pretty view, and Perennial Borders, as yet unplanted with a single perennial, that boasted a variety of trees and shrubs and, at that moment, also led nowhere. A start, but a wobbly one in many ways. But as we worked, we finally elected to believe principles are rules made to be, if not broken, certainly bent to fit unalterable circumstance. We now knew deeply that we would never have one of those astonishing geometric schemes one sees

surrounding the stateliest of European homes, with terraces and carved parterres and pleached allées gracefully transitioning into parkland. But again, we were not a stately European home. We were a charmingly wayward American farmstead; we would embrace all its eccentricities and challenges and, rather than trying to transform them, we would frame and celebrate them. And, with that bend-not-break-the-rules ethos firmly gripped in our now-calloused city-boy hands, off we went.

'Tardiva' hydrangeas in glorious bloom looking up to the Urn Garden in late summer.

OPPOSITE *Variegated box balls add nice architectural ballast running at intervals up the Pine & Dogwood Allée.*

Their fantastic spectrum of color and variegation makes hostas
indispensable for a shady planting—as long as deer aren't a problem.

HOSTAS

For all-season amiability, strength of show with equally engaging foliage and flower, and reliability in showing up year after year with scarcely a whine, it's hard to beat a hosta. The only down side? If you're not protected from deer, you're out of luck. Hostas are the manna of the plant world for that destructive intruder and, if you are not deer-fenced, in planting a bed of hosta, you might as well be opening a dessert bar. That said, if you have adequate protection, nothing enlivens a semi-shady to shady spot more brilliantly than the crisply striated, margined, swirled, and splotched (mainly with a brilliant white or yellow) leaves of hostas. Factor in that even the plainest cultivars boast a base foliage color that ranges from almost lemon-yellow through, as the Irish say, "a thousand shades of green" to dark purple and nearly true blue, and I believe we're onto something. We've planted hostas in many places at Hortulus Farm, not just the Birch Walk. In the Woodland Walk. The Dell. As a low, drifty understory in other wooded sectors. As a decorative border around the Herb Gardens and garnishing the north side of the corncrib. There are over 2,500 varieties of hosta so, as in so many cases, our advice will be to visit your local nursery and see what varieties they stock and recommend for your zone and site. Some say a rule of thumb is the paler the foliage, the happier they will be in some filtered sun, and the darker the foliage, the more they will prefer true shade. In any case, all are like cast iron once established, the only thing that might threaten them being a too-boggy spot for too long, which will make them rot, and the only grooming requirement being removing the spent flower spikes post-bloom. And, as if all that weren't sufficient recommendation, you can divide hostas and enlarge your real estate greatly over the years. We will leave you here with just a smattering of our favorite varieties on the farm.

» *Hosta* 'Blue Angel'

» *Hosta* 'Krossa Regal'

» *Hosta* 'Albomarginata'

» *Hosta sieboldiana* var. *elegans*

» *Hosta* 'Blue Umbrellas'

» *Hosta* 'Frances Williams'

» *Hosta* 'Sum and Substance'

» *Hosta sieboldii* 'Tiny Twister'

» *Hosta* 'Guacamole'

» *Hosta* 'Patriot'

» *Hosta* 'Halcyon'

» *Hosta* 'Aphrodite'

» *Hosta* 'Lime Zest'

» *Hosta* 'Sagae'

» *Hosta* 'Climax'

» *Hosta* 'Angel Falls'

A New Dawn

Between the 5th and 12th centuries, all hell broke loose on the Continent. The Roman Empire collapsed, and Europe was subsequently conquered and plundered by wave after wave of intruders, including the Visigoths, the Ostrogoths, the Huns (led by the winsome Attila), and the particularly unwelcome Viking and Magyar marauders of the 9th century. Finally and thankfully, beginning in the 12th century, order and intellect began the slow crawl to resurfacing, ultimately giving birth to the Renaissance in the 14th century, which saw a "rebirth" of the classical order that had been so sorely trampled under foot: a taming of nature and man's baser instincts into something refined, cerebral, distinguished and, above all, orderly, as described by the architectural and geometrically "golden" canons of earlier times. By the 16th century, as relative peace and a return to the creative possibilities of the human mind and spirit reigned on the European continent, the need for a defensive posture in architecture was happily on the wane and, all at once, people turned themselves around and began to look decoratively outward from where they dwelled into the surrounding countryside. It was then advised that new dwellings be raised on a higher elevation than the land surrounding them, not for defensive purposes but so that the elegant symmetry of classical garden design, which had begun to pervade greater Europe, could be viewed from above. Thus the parterre (literally, "on the ground") theory of gardening—in which rigidly symmetrical clipped box-edged beds were laid out like intricate Turkish carpets to delight the eye from on high—was born. Intricacy and order bordering on the obsessively meticulous and certainly ostentatious became the order of the day, with nature playing a completely subservient role to the machinations of human design.

 One of the most famous parterre gardens in the world is the formal potager at the Chateau de Villandry in France.

DO

Stand in each quadrant of the property surrounding your house and analyze its potential. If you are lucky enough to have a property of some acreage, the best thing to do is to identify the long views and garden "destinations." In many suburban cases, the yards on either side of a house will be narrow and in need of screening from neighbors, so it is the front and back that will, generally, be of greatest horticultural interest. In the front, wayfinding to the front door needs to lead the design. In the backyard, work to identify the existing topographical possibilities and optimal viewsheds.

Apply the age-old gardening tenet, whatever your property's size: the gardens nearest the house should reflect the architecture of the house to some extent and then become increasingly less formal as one moves away from the house.

Avail yourself of garden stakes and twine. Make a drawing of your aspired-to garden plan and then draw it on the ground with the stakes and twine. Here is the upper terrace. Here are the steps leading down to the orchard. Here is where the eight apple trees go. Here is the winding path to the vegetable garden and the garden itself. Here are the mixed borders. Here is the secret rose garden. The beauty of twine and stakes is you can adjust and readjust the plan until it all fits just right.

Honor the existing planting whenever possible, particularly your mature trees. We rarely counsel anyone to cut down a mature tree unless it is unsalvageably diseased or so shades the garden, further gardening is nearly impossible. And, even then, we are quick to recommend a shade garden. Trees are the great brutes and heroes of horticulture. Treat them with respect.

Identify areas of wetness or dryness and the quality of the soil in those precincts, as this will dictate where you will be headed in terms of planting. Also, are there rocky outcroppings that might be suitable for a rock garden idea? A natural slope that might be defined more attractively through the use of steps and terracing? Or would some compartmentalization through the use of hedging suddenly give your blank canvas some surprise and zing?

DON'T

Just take it all out so you can start with a blank canvas. On any property, save an already empty lot, there will surely be specimens worth saving and, just for instance, clear-cutting a wooded area will be a disservice to both your garden and yourself. Why on earth would you even purchase a house in such a situation if it wasn't what you desired? Embrace and work to enhance your home's specific sense of place, not destroy it.

Overlook borrowed views. Clearly, you will want some perimeter planting or even walls to shield you from your neighbors where they are too close by. However, if some aspect of your property gives onto a pastoral neighboring field or flashing creek or old churchyard or pretty sun-dappled wood, why not employ the view as a garden feature and enjoy any of those things visually without the necessity of their upkeep?

Fall into the trap of demanding full coverage as you begin your planting by placing plants, especially shrubs and trees, too close together. Analyze their full growth potential and plant accordingly. Yes, you may have to wait some years for your longed-for effect but that is far preferable to having to move now-substantial plant matter due to impatience.

Bow to rampant artificiality and artifice unless you are envisioning a miniature golf course as your longed-for environment. The well-placed piece of statuary or folly or water feature or garden shed as a desirable focal point is one thing. To populate your garden with an assortment of them will definitely be heading down the wrong primrose path. And don't make us say "jungle gym," "gargoyle," or "suncatcher."

On the other hand, don't be afraid to be yourself, armed with your full battery of eccentricities and likes and dislikes. If you want a scarecrow in the middle of your vegetable garden, have one. If you covet a rill, a grotto, or a stumpery, we say why not? If you are mad for lilies or hellebores or tulips, plant away, identifying a site and a scheme that will please both of you. Just try to keep those classical tenets and taste in mind. If you are in need of identifying the latter, feel free to contact us.

3

Hardscape—in the guise of terraces and stairways, garden houses and follies, fountains and watercourses, walls and statuary and focal points—has always held an important place in the horticultural lexicon, from the earliest

Land Crafting *& Hardscape*

Greek and Roman efforts onward. Land crafting is what Capability Brown, William Kent, and Humphry Repton unleashed in full upon the British landscape. Not that the introduction of fussy

The Urn Garden was the final gesture that completed the axis running from the Pool Garden up between the Summer Borders, through the Temple Canum, and up the Pine & Dogwood Allée.

parterred and terraced schemes with extravagant watercourses and acres of hardscape were natural to their precincts, but the sweeping away of all that and its replacement with newly wrought valleys and lakes and rushing rivers—real large-scale manipulation of the native topography—was a novelty not yet witnessed in England. Or elsewhere. Then, suddenly, the picturesque style of garden design was all the rage.

Dredging the Lake

We have really done an absolute minimum of land crafting on the
farm but, nearly as soon as we arrived in 1979, we plunged right into
the first bit. We had inherited from the previous owners a map of the
original acreage that included a "lake"—a free-form, crosshatched,
amoeba shape on the map that had clearly been the result of some
previous owner damming up the creek, so that the lake ultimately
spilled over a dam to rejoin the creek beneath the little bridge on
the drive that spanned it. But there was no lake there—just a massive,
boggy, saplinged-in depression, which, while still flowing over the
dam to some extent, left the creek, which should have been burbling
away downslope from the house, nearly dry. The first parcel of land
we acquired in our first year on the farm was happily the 30 acres
directly west of the original 15 acres, which included a good half of
the amoeba labeled "lake." So here, finally, was a gesture—a decisive,
spirit-lifting, classically inspired, Capability Brown of a gesture—we
could leap on without trepidation, feet first, all four firmly in motion.

Therefore, spring 1980 heralded the arrival of a large yellow
backhoe, a dump truck, and their owner, our neighbor, who rented
himself out with his battery of heavy equipment despite the fact
that he had inherited his family farm with about 200 acres of prime
country real estate less than a mile down the road. This was a typical
rural Bucks County tale, at least in our early days there: slightly more
than subsistence farmers, mainly Quakers, sitting on vast tracts of land
their families had farmed for generations and doing what they had
been raised to do, generally growing soy or corn or wheat or raising
cattle or chickens or swine, working hard, worshipping on Sundays in
one of the handsome 18th-century stone meeting houses that were
the jewels in the crown of every tiny town and hamlet (along with
an equally seasoned local tavern), and never wanting more or less.
That many of these farmsteads, which truly seemed to exist out of
time, would all too soon fall prey to developers, whose McMansion
anti-style would prove totally unsympathetic to the sturdy simplicity
of the Quaker ethos, is one of the tragedies we have witnessed in our
neighborhood in our 40 years on the farm. But that, as they say, is
another story.

TOP *Our Japanese
teahouse, crafted in faux
bois, is just one example
of the sharpening
effect and visual focus
hardscape can bring to
a garden.*

BELOW *Some of our
ducks and geese in
winter looking across
the lake to the stone
pier and the steps up
to Bacchus and the
Bluebell Lake.*

As our neighbor set to work, scooping up bucketloads of muck and saplings to be deposited in the rear of the dump truck and hauled away, we discovered something interesting: a large concrete plug buried deep in the overgrowth that, when removed, caused the soupy bog to drain just like pulling the plug in a bathtub, making the rest of the clearing and excavation a relative piece of cake. In a matter of weeks, we had re-dug the lake to the boundaries indicated on the map to a central depth of about 8 feet. We also lined the southern bank of the lake with a stout stone retaining wall, as we surmised that it had been the spring runoff down the slope from the

The Temple Canum lies at the bottom of the Pine & Dogwood Allée and at the top of the steep, concave slope (soon to be the Summer Borders) we excavated to flatten the pool plateau.

current nursery operation that had filled in the lake to begin with. In any event, we replaced the plug and waited with some impatience for Fire Creek to refill the now-immense hole in the ground. As it transpired, the lake also proved to be spring fed to some extent. So, in a matter of weeks, the lake, an oval-esque idea approximately 30 feet wide by 50 feet long, was filled and cascading prettily over the dam and under the drive to rejoin the creek running east, which now flowed most appealingly below the house. Capability Brown would have been very proud.

The Pool Plateau
and Summer Borders

The second and only other piece of major land crafting we realized
on the farm was the leveling of the pool plateau for the circular Pool
Garden as the visual destination at the end of the Perennial Borders.
This was a relatively simple exercise involving the removal of earth
from the north side of that northern slope down to the creek and

*The pool plateau is by
far the largest, flattest
piece of turf on the
entire farm.*

the dumping of it to the south to, ultimately, create a perfectly flat circular plain about 130 feet in circumference. It had already been a flattish affair, as it was really an extension of that west to east axis that runs up the driveway and out the Perennial Borders between the barns. So, in the end, on the upslope side, where we had cut into the slope with some vengeance, there stood a steep, concave crescent of naked soil and, on the downslope side, a rather more gentle drop-off to the slope continuing down to the creek. As that upslope cut stood bare to the sun in what had been essentially treeless pasture, another,

The Summer Borders were our brilliantly colored solution to that steep, concave bank on the north side of the pool plateau.

brighter border idea hatched and, on that sunny, south-facing slope, the Summer Borders came into being—a massive gesture of brightly hued trees, shrubs, perennials, and bamboos and other grasses. The downslope edge we planted with deep red Japanese maples and blue hydrangeas and surrounded the whole plateau with a sextet of immense American holly sentinels.

We have already referenced the Pine & Dogwood Allée as the long, south to north axis that climbs that northern slope from the pool to, ultimately, achieve the yet-to-be-conceived Urn Garden, although the pool plateau was instituted considerably in advance of both of those ideas. However, once all three were in place, it quickly became apparent there needed to some way to access the new allée from the pool plateau. There happened to be a native dogwood dead

center at the top of the then-single Summer Border, so we bisected it and ran a turf path up from the pool to the dogwood, and, behind it, the entrance to the new allée. It then became apparent that some transitional hardscape was needed to add definition and coherence to this new plan, so we surrounded the dogwood with an antique iron tree bench, created an oval, stone-edged gravel terrace for it, and further flanked that with two semicircular classical arcades grown with wisteria and a pair of dog statues on plinths.

We have always loved the idea of the canine burial plots one so often sees in English gardens, and this was destined to become ours, what we call the Temple Canum: each of our past darlings having a river stone with his or her name inscribed on it beneath the tree bench. In our 40 years on the farm, we have adopted

The southern lip of the pool plateau is planted with a course of Japanese maples that are particularly brilliant in fall.

upward of a dozen dogs from local shelters. They are our children, and we can say without hesitation that nothing in our lives has been more emotionally rewarding than they have, or reflected so much unconditional love in our direction. If you have never rescued a dog from a shelter, do not hesitate for another second. We currently have Bandit, Sadie, and Parker (Medium Mix/Wheaton Terrier/Small Mix) as well as three rescue horses (Smokey, Miley, and Petunia), two adopted sheep (Nancy and Debo), two adopted pygmy goats (Virginia and Vanessa), a good number of adopted pigeons and doves, two peacocks (Charles and Camilla), a chicken house full of chickens, a barn cat (T.J.) and a lakeful of ducks, geese, and swans. The farm wouldn't be the same without them. In our opinion, especially in a situation replete with stalls and paddocks, flora is fine, but it is nothing without fauna.

We have had many rescue dogs over the years and, like Bandit and Parker here, they have enriched our lives beyond measure.

OPPOSITE LEFT
The statues on the plinths flanking the Temple Canum look just like our beloved hound Chester.

OPPOSITE RIGHT
Without the elemental sounds of animal life, particularly the chickens, roosters, geese, ducks, and peacocks, the farm would be a very hollow place indeed.

OPPOSITE BELOW
Our old boy, Smokey, a study in grays and with the sweetest disposition.

Hardscape

Gardens are really described as much by their hardscape as by their plantings. Steps and terracing, fencing, stone edging, and pathways sharpen the natural topography of the garden, giving it shape and order. Hard architecture not only organizes and adds ballast to a garden but also provides a wonderful counterpoint to the soft, blowsy charms of plant life. Luckily, we started with our substantial architecture—stone farmhouse, barns, corncrib, chicken house, mother-in-law house, milk barn—at the heart of the farm to anchor the plantings that radiate from it, plus a healthy swath of post and rail fencing scrawling itself across fields, defining pastures. But we still had acres of lawn and soon-to-be gardens that begged for some definition and counterpoint to their defiant asymmetry and general rowdiness.

In Bucks County, stone is definitely the material of choice for almost anything and, most significantly, for the plethora of elegantly simple 18th-century meeting houses, taverns, and dwellings like ours that populate our area. As well, quarries are still a part of nearly every Bucks County township. Therefore, stone walls, steps, and foundations were our choices, almost entirely, in terms of hardscape, lending not only a really substantial organizational component to the gardens but a becoming cohesion as well.

We've noted the stone retaining wall the holds the south bank of the lake but not the stone pier we built out into the lake that joins with it, nor the semicircular stone steps and pillars leading up from the Woodland Walk on the south side to the Bluebell Lake or the ones that mirror them that complete the Counselor's Circle across the lake on the downslope edge. We've discussed the hefty stone foundation we built for the Temple Canum at the bottom of the Pine & Dogwood Allée, but not the one we constructed for the 12-foot urn that is the visual destination at the top, or the massive set of stone steps at the very top of the Birch Walk (really the entrance to the gardens as one descends from the nursery), or the three sets of steps composed of old, handhewn Philadelphia curbstones that climb the steep bank chopped into the hillside across the drive from the house.

At the top of that embankment, planted when we arrived with vinca and a huge run of forsythia, now resides our Kitchen Garden

OPPOSITE *Raised beds and vertical structure add much-needed organization and architecture to the Kitchen Garden.*

OVERLEAF *Our stately dairy barns along with the stone farmhouse are the real anchors of the gardens on the farm.*

and, beyond that, the mother-in-law house. However, there was no way to access the ground at the top without walking to one end of the embankment or the other, where it finally met the natural topography of the hill canting down into the valley, so the three sets of steps were implemented. The westernmost set leads to the aviary, Cutting Round, and the west gate of the Kitchen Garden, the middle set to the south gate of the Kitchen Garden, and the easternmost set to the Herb Gardens, chicken house, and Edible Rooms. They all climb that embankment in the most nonchalant way, the westernmost curving slightly to achieve the summit with the Cutting Round as its visual destination, the middle one fairly straight up to the central southern gate of the Kitchen Garden, both of these flanked by staggered ranks of dwarf Alberta spruce, and the easternmost quite broad with the top step on absolute axis with the viewshed leading up to the Herb Gardens and Edible Rooms. Not only do they add much-needed definition to that slope but, also, the easy access necessary for the keeping of herb, vegetable, and cutting gardens.

We inherited most of the post and rail fencing that describes our various paddocks and pastures and feel it strikes exactly the right "farm appropriate" note.

OPPOSITE *The westernmost set of ex-Philadelphia curbstone steps, planted with dwarf Alberta spruce, leading up to the aviary and Cutting Round.*

The Terraces

When we first arrived at the farm, the house sat on a grassy slope about 15 feet above Fire Creek most notable for three stately trees: a tulip magnolia, an American elm, and an immense Japanese maple, the first and last we assume planted by the Fravels in the late 1930s. We lost the maple to old age about five years ago (we've planted a replacement) and the elm to Dutch elm disease just this past year. Almost half the tulip magnolia was lost to Hurricane Sandy, but it has triumphantly resurged to fight another day. The view overlooking the creek and milk pond and, to the right, the lake as one looks down from the house is a very pastoral idea indeed and one we were intent on celebrating. To that end, we hit upon the idea of a set of

stone terraces, one leading down to the other, then down the slope to the creek, to serve as an outdoor living room of sorts and, also, as a showcase for some of our potted tropicals from the nursery in summer. Both terraces are constructed of random local flagstone with spaces in between, welcoming to mosses and sedum. The upper terrace, a rectangular affair some 50 feet long and 15 feet wide, runs the length of the house and can be accessed from the east or west, where it meets the natural incline of the slope, or from a steep set of steps from the porch. It has a central set of semicircular steps leading down to the lawn.

The lower terrace, another rectangle about 15 feet by 35 feet, is accessed by a set of steps from the upper terrace on the west side, with yet another set of steps leading down to the lawn. Both terraces

By bringing out many of our potted tender and tropical plants from the nursery to display on the terraces in summer, we hope to engage visitors in the charms of these interesting and unusual specimens.

are populated with a collection of antique iron garden chairs, tables, and benches, all painted a light French blue, and this is where garden clubs who request a tour with boxed lunch happily dine following their tour—we can seat about 50, which is a handy busful.

Focal Points and Visual Destinations

Focal points usually occur either in the middle of a garden as a central feature or at the end of a vista as a visual destination. As we meander through the woodland around the lake, for instance, we can identify several examples of focal point. First, as one descends to the Woodland Walk from the Birch Walk, one views the totem of one of James Fuhrman's sculptures, then the focal point of the pavilion floating on the lake, then, as one swivels left along the woodland path and up that set of stone steps on the southside, the intense surprise of Bacchus rising from his Bluebell Lake. Descending to the creek, the visual destinations are of the fanciful twig bridge spanning it and the rustic teahouse anchoring the northwestern slope as one crosses to the north side. Moving now east, one enters the Yellow & Variegated Foliage Garden with its central stand of golden locusts. Then, climbing northward, there's the symmetrical surprise of the Counselor's Circle with its variegated dogwood and tree bench at the center. Continuing westward along the northern path, one encounters the swirling bird at the center of the Topiary Garden and another Fuhrman sculpture, each in its own little clearing. As noted, these are, in the main, central focal point ideas. Other examples of central focal points on the farm are the Eiffel Tower in the French Garden, the pool and fountain in the pool plateau, the poncirus tree in the Edible Rooms, the village fountain in the Mediterranean Garden, the sundial in the Herb Gardens, and the apple pavilion that anchors the Kitchen Garden.

We've already discussed the siting of the Italian tazza at the dogleg in the Birch Walk, so that it's the visual destination from both

James Fuhrman's "Reflections of a Quiet Mind" is the visual destination at the bottom of the Birch Walk.

top and bottom. The Urn Garden as the visual destination at the top of the Pine & Dogwood Allée involved the acquisition of another major statement piece. Clearly, much like the majestic statue of Hercules that caps the grand allée at Vaux-le-Vicomte in France, we were in need of something truly substantial to catch the eye. We have a friend who does major seasonal installations at some of the casinos in Las Vegas, among other far-flung venues, and he was anxious to de-access a 12-foot-tall aluminum urn made in Mexico that had danced at one of his installations. As urns seem to fit seamlessly and even classically into most garden schemes, even on such a massive scale, we said "you bet," because, in a nutshell, such scale was exactly what the situation called for. We're talking an allée of more than 300 feet moving upslope with this thing vaguely at the top. So we built it a big, square stone plinth with planting pockets to give it even more substantiality, had a faux-painter friend of ours come to give it some weathered bronze patina, and planted away with vitex, hydrangeas, variegated box balls, and climbing roses, with a quartet of fastigiate copper beeches anchoring each corner and, further out, a quartet

The twig bridge, composed of mountain laurel, is the surprising visual destination as one descends to the creek along the Woodland Walk.

OPPOSITE *Bacchus, with the support of Pan, raises his dish of wine in the middle of the Bluebell Lake.*

*Another of James
Fuhrman's steel
sculptures, the very
organic "Akebono,"
resides in a circular
clearing on the north
side of the
Woodland Walk.*

OPPOSITE *The
miniature of the Eiffel
Tower, which, oddly,
we purchased in the
English Cotswolds, is
the centerpiece of the
French Garden.*

of cunninghamias to give it even more heft and importance. It now
makes a profound visual statement even from the Temple Canum at
the bottom of the allée, and, from its position on the highest point
on the property, one can also look across the Lajeski Meadow to the
Windybush Valley, so beloved of the Bucks County Impressionist
painters, and beyond. It's a glorious view—our only really long one
into the surrounding countryside—and this borrowed vista, while it
was one we had no hand in making, is surely one for which we are
profoundly thankful.

HARDSCAPE CONSIDERATIONS

While we have been romancing the virtues of native Pennsylvania stone as a hardscape material of vernacular suitability and endless possibility in this chapter, it is far from the only material we have employed in our efforts on the farm. First of all, there's brick and block, too. Or take, for instance, the possibilities of timber and even man-made timber-esque ideas. We've already mentioned the huge amount of post and rail fencing we have on the farm. But, of course, you can craft many personalities of fence from timber, from stockade to board-and-batten and picket. Here we will also put in a good word for composite wood: lengths crafted of sawdust and resin that walk the wooden walk and are perfect for some types of fencing, raised garden beds, etc. After losing far too many to rot, we now fashion the pickets for the Kitchen Garden fence out of composite: when painted, it is absolutely undetectable and virtually indestructible. As well, in the Kitchen Garden, hefty, pressure-treated 8 by 8s define the raised beds, and in the Woodland Walk, the creek is spanned by a twig bridge with a pressure-treated wooden deck and a framework constructed of mountain laurel. Across from the Birch Walk, steps composed of substantial logs packed with dirt lead up to the back of Bluebell Lake and the Woodland Walk. And we have endless paths of chipped timber,

✳ Hardscape is indispensable for adding both organizational architecture and complementary texture to a garden.

most of it of our own manufacture from whatever is down in the woods, scrolling their way through the Dell and woodlands, connecting one garden with another and, also, creating what we lovingly term "I-95," the service paths that allow us to drive our golf carts (fitted with cargo boxes at the back) wherever they are needed. And, finally, we'll return to stone and the extremely useful idea of pea gravel, which, with an underlayment of shade cloth, is perfect for more decorative paths like the ones in the Kitchen Garden and Edible Rooms.

And here we add just one more renegade note: classicism and appropriateness is all well and good, but what about the introduction of something wildly at odds with its surroundings as a focal point or statement? What about all that wonderful juxtaposition one finds in gardens that host sculpture exhibitions or, better, permanent installations, these creating that slight friction that sometimes results in the most surprising success? A fabulous collection of kinetic George Rickeys or a herd of Elisabeth Frink's horses stampeding across a parkland with a Georgian folly and cascade as the central feature? Or the beauty of a single Henry Moore or Barbara Hepworth decorating the broad lawn of the stateliest of English manors? Which is why we have hosted an annual sculpture display in the gardens for the past several years, these embracing many personalities, a single artist per season. It adds excitement and novelty and embraces the present moment. It begs for interaction and opinion. All this is good for a garden. Ultimately, have we managed to achieve the correct aesthetic balance and note? We believe so but, honestly, you will have to come visit and be the judge.

Looking across the paddocks of the beautiful dressage facility that neighbors us to the east to the Windybush Valley.

 The parterre school of garden design, these at the Belvedere Palace garden in Vienna.

PARTERRES
for All

Although the parterre idea is clearly a French designation, initially this style of gardening was referred to as Italianate. This, of course, made perfect sense as all those classically "golden" formulas of geometry and ideal spatial relationship, from the height and breadth of buildings to the correct relationship between step and riser, were originally Greek or Roman, and the Italian peninsula was littered with ancient examples of the formulas in action. Soon enough, however, the Italian style made its way from the Mediterranean region and became firmly entrenched in France as the "garden à la française," and the parterre became its horticultural signature. By the early 16th century, this garden scheme had found its way across the Channel into Great Britain, there to be bolstered in the next century (with the arrival of the Dutch-born king of England, Ireland, and Scotland, William III) by the even more fastidious and orderly Dutch style of gardening. Perhaps because the Netherlands is such a petite piece of turf, severely linear Dutch gardens were renowned for their chock-a-block use of space, surrounded by clipped hedging and always densely planted and so intensively organized (think regiments of colorful tulips cheek by jowl) as to verge on the obsessive. In 1896, Gertrude Jekyll commented thusly on this period in English gardening: "They remained faithful to the old traditions, of parterre and bowling-green, pleached alley, turfed walk, and clipped hedge, with certain additions derived from foreign influence, those from France inclining to increased stateliness and importance, and those from Holland to an extreme rigidity of treatment, with various matters of petty detail."

DO

Absorb the idea that land crafting and hardscape go hand in hand like Dick and Jane traveling up the hill with their blueberry buckets and that they should be considered together, as a single, messy, undoubtedly headache-making and purse-gouging but necessary starting point to any garden. Bite the bullet, open up your wallet, bring in the big machines all at once, and get the whole tedious business done with.

Try to keep land crafting to a minimum. Not only is it expensive and time-consuming—and did we mention messy?—but, rather than change it, what we really urge you to do is try and embrace the eccentricities of your property as we have done with ours. Tax your imagination and look for inventive ways to celebrate its quirks and make them part of what makes your patch of land uniquely personal.

Introduce *some* hardscape into your garden scheme. Hardscape is really the great enhancer of plant material. Its steadfast, well, "hardness," we suppose, is the perfect foil for the more spontaneous charms of plant matter. For instance, edging a border with Belgian block gives it instant order, even as the perennials spill over it. Or a central set of stone steps anchoring a grassy knoll will direct the eye in exactly the right way to your focal point at the bottom (or top) and also provide just the right bit of architecture. Think about it.

Shop around for ideas in terms of hardscape. There are many other ideas we haven't touched on, from wrought and cast iron or other metals to PVC (frankly, we are not big fans, but if you need a carefree, white privacy fence further masked with planting, it's a consideration). Any big box store will have a whole range of possibilities. Do, however, as in all things, let conscience and taste be your guide.

Visit some local or even non-local gardens that seem of interest, before you make these kinds of decisions. If you have a strong local vernacular as we do (Quaker, 18th century), see what other people have done with a home of similar feeling, including hardscape as well as plant matter choices. If your local aesthetic cries out for pickets or wrought iron or board-and-batten, perhaps that's something to consider.

DON'T

Try to severely alter the lay of your land. The land has taken on its native geography and topographical eccentricities for very specific reasons. First of all, that's what the glacier, as it ran off, left behind. Then, that is where the sun shines. That is where the water flows. That is where the soil is rich, or not. Here is where to build a house. These things were done for a reason or, simply, this is what the story is. Ignorance is foolish. Listen up.

Take the easy way out. Go for as much quality as you can possibly afford, even if it means accomplishing your garden in stages. In the long run, you will be glad you did. "Settling for" and "cheaping out" will only come back to bite you in the end: things will fall apart. Finishes will degrade. And, if things are not installed properly, that will come back to bite you, too. Garden hardscape needs to be built to last. As in so many circumstances, "cheap" will never age to be anything else.

Even think of heading in the direction of those ubiquitous composite concrete building blocks, usually in shades of gray or "brick-ish," mountains of which usually reside outside the nursery area of the box stores. Honestly, we would have to hang our heads in shame and surrender our horticultural identification cards if we had ever succumbed. Head instead over to some real stuff: brick or Belgian block or stacked stone. This is a taste thing. 'Nuff said.

Try to install it yourself if you have no idea what you're doing. Installing brickwork or stacked stonewalls or board-and-batten fencing requires specific experience and knowledge (again, as in so many circumstances). Walls need to be canted. Posts need to be anchored in concrete. These things are best left to the professionals.

Mix too many metaphors unless you want to be headed down that slippery slope to Miniature Golfville. Identify a style or vernacular and stick with it. This all has to do, of course, with the architecture of your house. Colonial? Baronial? Mediterranean? Southern Charm? Does it scream for pickets or post and rail? Brick or flagstone? The severely modern or the gracefully aged? Let your home take the lead in terms of vernacular and materials.

4

Water
Features

One of the siltation ponds we dug at the western end of the lake doing what water features do best: mirroring their surroundings and the sky above.

Water features are a profound gift to a garden. Visually, they provide a shimmering, reflective counterpoint to greenery, ponds and lakes especially being so beautifully ephemeral in their ability to change personality entirely with shifts in the color of the sky, the wind, and weather, yet always taking on that mirror-like quality that, like a piece of magic in the landscape, doubles your view in mirror image while also capturing the movement of clouds and the dazzle of sun above. Aurally, they provide a whole symphony of soothing sound, from the *basso* whoosh of a waterfall to the humming melodic line of a steadily flowing stream to the bell-like tinklings of fountains as they cascade into their basins.

Every garden should have a water feature, even if it's just a decorative birdbath to reflect the sky and bring avian life into the garden. We're lucky enough to have an assortment of water features on the farm, some of Mother Nature's manufacture, some created or trucked in by us, but all, dotted about our 30 acres of gardens, doing exactly what they need to do: elevate one's sensory experience as one discovers the gardens.

The Creek and Lake

Mother Nature, of course, created the creek. We have no idea why it is evocatively called Fire Creek, only guessing that perhaps there was

Aside from the lake, certainly our most prominent water feature is the anything-but-ordinary swimming pool, acting as both visual destination and focal point.

OVERLEAF *One can just glimpse (and almost hear) the falls at the eastern end of the lake beneath the driveway bridge that spans the creek, here adorned with purple wisteria in spring.*

a forge on it sometime in the 17th or 18th century, and we're equally unsure as to where exactly its headwaters reside, as Bucks County boasts an astonishing abundance of creeks and streams, all somewhat randomly interconnected, over 50 named ones in all. Suffice it to say Fire Creek runs west to east through the farm and, at some moment east of us, must surely empty via some tributary or other into the Delaware River. It's torrential only in spring (or during a particularly heavy rainfall), when the runoff streams on the north and south flanks kick into high gear with the melting of the snows and it seems like the creek is intent on ripping away its banks as well as depositing whatever it is carrying along with it at the west end of the lake. To solve that problem, we dug two small siltation ponds in the woodland at the western end with the twig bridge spanning the creek between the two. These are far easier to dredge than having to

The view of the lake and lake pavilion looking east from the Yellow & Variegated Foliage Garden.

OPPOSITE *Fire Creek running placidly below the house on a fine spring afternoon with the little milk pond just to the right across that narrow bank.*

pull the plug on the lake to remove excess rubble. Most of the time, the creek is gently flowing, tumbling prettily over the dam at the east end of the lake, then under the bridge on the drive to rejoin itself as it continues its placid journey below the house and lower barn. In a drought season, it may be reduced to a trickle by August but, in the main, it's a shimmering ribbon broken by boulders and patches of iris meandering its way through the bottom of the farm. We added a second stone and turf bridge below and just to the east of the house to cross over the creek to a "secret" garden by the milk pond.

We have discussed the dredging and replenishing of the lake. It is such an intrinsic part of our landscape at this point that, honestly, we can't really remember when it wasn't there. It's the first major thing our guests see at the bottom of the Birch Walk when they come to tour, as well as the centerpiece of the first part of any tour, which involves circumlocuting the lake on the Woodland Walk. What we have not discussed is the lake pavilion we constructed when we had emptied the lake for dredging. Renny was keen that there be some architectural construct to catch and focus the eye across the lake as one reached the bottom of the Birch Walk. We discussed what amounted to a New England–style boathouse and dock, such as one might see on Cape Cod, but ended up with the idea of a vaguely Victorian, peak-roofed pavilion reached by a gangplank from the middle of the northern shore, capping a substantial octagonal deck. The plan was to roof the structure with cedar shakes but, when we saw it with just the lattice structure in place, we loved the airiness of it and elected to stop there. Painted a crisp white, the pavilion is the focal point of the lake, geese and ducks and swans gliding by, adding their own bit of romance, as it forever kisses its reflection in the placid waters upon which it rides.

One of our beautiful Australian black swans, this the very friendly and always-glad-to-check-in-with-you male.

The Milk Pond

The milk pond, directly downslope and across the creek from the house, was man-made in the 19th century when the Warner/Thompsons turned to the dairy business. It was built to keep the canisters of milk the farm produced cool in the heat of summer and was neighbored to the east by a low stone ice house, of which we have an early photo but which had completely disappeared by the time we arrived on the scene. The eastern end of the pond is now the site of a "secret" garden: a cloistered, green, ferny affair anchored by an absolutely massive antique stone bench and perfect for illicit trysts and such—and who couldn't use a few more of those? The pond is filled via a pipe running underground beneath the drive from the lake, then it, in turn, is re-piped when full back into the creek running just beneath it to the north. Our biggest issue is the bank separating pond from creek. When we first arrived, the bank

The boggy, nonreflective soup of the milk pond after the bank was breached this spring: it's always something, right?

was perhaps 8 feet broad at the top, with a path one could stroll to reach the secret garden. However, over the years, as the creek has run torrentially in spring, it has severely eroded that northern bank to a scant 3 feet across, and even that dimension is questionable in spots. Needless to say, there is no more path, as one is in dire danger of either falling into the pond on one side or the creek on the other.

Despite our best efforts, including a significant dumping of boulders and the planting of substantial grasses to hold the bank, we seem to be facing a losing battle. This past season, we had 8 inches of rain in six hours, and the creek rose by 6 feet, rushing over both the driveway and bridge below the house, carrying a heavy teak bench from the stone pier on the lake to be deposited in three pieces below the pool plateau, and creating a massive breach in the milk pond wall. We're considering options as we write, including repairing and reinforcing the wall. Another option is simply to finally remove the wall and allow the creek to repossess that real estate.

Sedum, evening primroses, wild carnations, and ornamental grasses, among others, decorate the Pool Garden's heat-loving rock garden surround.

OPPOSITE *The pool fountain is right on the edge of farmstead appropriateness, but we feel it just makes the cut.*

The Pool Garden

We conceived the pool plateau specifically to create a flat, circular plain into which we could inset our pool, which would do triple duty as the centerpiece of that space; as the visual destination at the end of the Perennial Borders and at the bottom of the Pine & Dogwood Allée and Summer Borders; and, finally, as an actual

swimming pool. We knew we wanted a swimming pool but not of the typical rectangular, aqua-tinted, diving-boarded type situated in unsympathetic proximity to the house. For one thing, no flat area remotely near the house was large enough to accommodate a pool. And, in any case, we wanted the pool to present itself as a garden feature, not a flagrantly inappropriate piece of hardscape begging for discreet enclosure. So Renny conceived the idea of a round pool, 30 feet in diameter, surfaced in black with a central fountain and a discreet set of steps at the shallow western end grading to a depth of 6 feet at the eastern deep end, the whole surrounded by a simple flagstone coping. The fountain, a classically inspired affair 6 feet tall with a shallow basin help aloft by a trio of putti, was actually not a fountain at all when we discovered it at a local salvage and garden antiques yard but, in effect, a huge birdbath, with no piping for a water source. We purchased it and, with a good deal of concern, had the central column around which the putti disported themselves

Our single purpose in the design and siting of our swimming pool was to disguise it as a garden feature.

OPPOSITE *The rock garden surrounding the pool was an afterthought that resulted in what we consider one of our most successful gardens.*

drilled to accommodate a pipe, fearing all the while that it might split in two as a result of such intrusion. It did not. We built a central, mortared stone plinth linked to the pool recycling mechanism rising to a height of 18 inches above water level, then hooked the fountain up on top of it. Now, as the pool water recirculates, water spills over the sides of the basin and cascades down, back into the pool. A feature appropriate to an American farm vernacular? We're pleading the Fifth.

The rock garden surround for the Pool Garden was really an afterthought. Until about 15 years ago, the turf of the pool plateau directly abutted the pool's stone coping, the only horticultural note consisting of six standard PeeGee hydrangeas underplanted with bergenia evenly spaced around the circumference. It was a tidy look

The sextet of PeeGee hydrangeas that ring the Pool Garden come into glorious bloom in August.

but lacked sparkle and, as the pool lies absolutely naked to the sun, it occurred to Renny that if we extended the stone coping by about a yard, laying the pavers in sand, we could plant a heat-loving rock garden, which is exactly what we did. In the main, the stones are carpeted with creeping thyme and low-growing 'Weihenstephaner Gold' sedum as well as a long run of cotoneaster tumbling over the lip of the pool at the deep end. To that carpet, however, we added two 'Gold Mound' spireas, stands of miniature iris, oxeye daisies, evening primrose, 'Elijah Blue' fescue, more bergenias, cinquefoils, and wild carnations, many of which have self-seeded over time.

The result is a very sprightly midsummer picture, with the thyme in purple bloom and the sedum almost electric with acid-yellow blossom, the deep, Schiaparelli pink of the carnations, the

<hr />

sunny yellow cinquefoils, the soft, soft pink of the evening primroses, the purple-blue of the irises, and the yellow and white of the daisies all contributing to a really pretty show. Then, of course, the hydrangeas provide their extravagant blossom in the late summer, several of these surrounded with a bright carpeting of black-eyed Susans, which come into bloom at the same moment. We should also mention here the stone-pillared gloriette with a fanciful ironwork top at the southern lip of the pool plateau which provides shade for a small luncheon table beneath it. This we have grown with yellow climbing rose, golden hops vine, trumpet vine, and the beguilingly splotched 'Mint Crisp' honeysuckle, creating a wild, dense green canopy of shade looping through the ironwork, dotted with interesting foliage and parti-colored blossom, all set against the curving rank of Japanese maples at the plateau's edge.

The Village Fountain

The Mediterranean Garden, a circular garden in the northeast corner of the farm in what was former cow pasture, is achieved in two ways: by a lane of goldenrain trees that radiates from above the Temple Canum to the right and, also, by a path mown into the Lajeski Meadow extending sinuously down from the Urn Garden at the top of the Pine & Dogwood Allée. It is entirely encircled by a ring of 'Nana Variegata' weigelas and, especially from the Lajeski Meadow, it comes as a nearly complete surprise as one enters a breach in the weigela hedge. Its centerpiece is a carved stone affair we think of as an Italian village fountain, although we purchased it in France, in Houdan, a town near Versailles. One would think it was ancient, but it was, in fact, newly wrought when we chanced upon it some

On a misty morning from the Lajeski Meadow, one looks down on the mystery of the circle of 'Nana Variegata' weigelas that encloses the Mediterranean Garden.

30 years ago. It consists of an octagonal basin with a center column sprouting four iron spouts that prettily deliver water into the basin. It danced at one of our installations at the Philadelphia Flower Show in the 1990s inside the iron and stone gloriette (bought on the same trip to Houdan) that now provides shade on the pool plateau. As the closest natural water source is the creek at the very bottom of the Lajeski Meadow's slope, this is definitely a recirculating idea. Surely, the whole affair is one of those conceits on the farm that runs the risk of crossing that "farm appropriate" line into no-no land but, again, we have sited it so spontaneously and it is approached so informally that, somehow, we think it works. In any case, it's awfully nice to chance upon the sparkle and tinkle of this cloistered moment on a pastoral hillside in rural Pennsylvania. We'll talk specifically about the Mediterranean Garden's themed plantings and garden inspirations in Chapter 8.

The sound and look of the village fountain at the center of the Mediterranean Garden transport one to a place very far away from a Pennsylvania hillside.

The Koi Pond

The koi pond, inset into the lower terrace of the house, is another recirculating water feature. We bought the antique, bull-nosed stone coping that surrounds it extremely early on in our tenancy at a salvage yard, it forming a rectangle about 4 feet by 6 feet, and, for many years, it sat in pieces in the work area of our woods, where we keep our piles of stone and gravel and split wood and compost for future use. We almost forgot about it but not quite. We had built the upper terrace and were fairly content with that arrangement until we put two and two together and had the bright idea to build a further, lower terrace offset to the west of the upper terrace, specifically for the addition of the koi pond. We faced the interior of the pond with mortar and river stone, installed the salvaged coping in the flag terrace, and added a lead turtle to sit on the coping and spout water back into the pond. We stocked it with flashing koi and a big pot of papyrus and, for many years, it was a stalwart addition to that view down from the house across the terraces to the lake across the drive. However, it began to leak about five years ago and, despite our best

SWIMMING POOLS

S wimming pools are anathema to garden design and everyone has to have one. A brilliant aqua rectangle set in a frame of concrete with a diving board at one end and some chaises for sunning and perhaps a patio dining set at the other. Just add the swing set, the children, and the grill replete with sassily aproned grill-meister, and you have everything that makes us want to enter horticultural witness protection. However, there is hope here, but only if you will put down your beer pong paddles and listen. Because the truth is, you can have your pool and love it, too. First of all, think of it as a garden feature that just happens to allow you to float about with a paper parasol in your glass of a summer's afternoon. Secondly, it doesn't have to be aqua. It doesn't have to be rectangular. It doesn't need to have a diving board or even a handrail. And it certainly doesn't need to have a concrete slab surrounding it. Now, we realize that in many cases, local ordinances will decree a childproof fence entirely surround your pool but this, in a way, can be your savior. In many precincts, they need to be 4 to 5 feet high, which is a perfect cue for some green hedging or classic wooden fencing with a perennial border decorating it on the house side that will, at the same moment, shield it from view. And why not make it round or square and paint the interior deep blue or black, or cover it in fairytale-like iridescent tiles to sparkle in the sun? And why not surround it with a patio of flag or brick or coral stone, or just plain turf with no coping but with planting pockets dotted about, these last large enough for trees, shrubs, and perennials (and, of course, sufficient downtime sunny space for the chaises. And shade for the dining spot. All right: and grill . . .). This could be a transformative idea. But no sassy aprons, okay? A deal's a deal.

efforts to identify the leak in the mortar and river stone interior and multiple visits from the local stonemason as well as applications of sealer, it defied us until just this season when, with multiple applications of a new sealer, we have achieved wholeness. We just restocked it with infant koi and are thrilled to see them flashing and darting through its depths again.

A koi pond, with the antique stone coping we bought at salvage, is the centerpiece of the lower terrace.

 William Kent and Capability Brown were the authors of the picturesque school, which swept artificiality and ostentation away to be replaced by the naturalistic.

The Picturesque
SCHOOL

Finally, in the mid-1700s, before the manipulative hands of the British ruling classes, armed with their Continental conceits plucked from the French, Italian, and Dutch vernacular, managed to erase all that was natural and organic from the English countryside, enter the legendary British garden architects William Kent (master importer of the Palladian style) and, in the next generation, Lancelot "Capability" Brown, the father of landscape architecture. Kent's most famous garden achievement is surely the Arcadian park at Stowe, with its vast and serenely rolling landscape dotted with lakes, cascades, grottoes, bridges, and classically inspired temples, with not a jot of symmetry or linear orderliness in sight. Later in the same century, Capability Brown picked up the picturesque baton and brought it to its fullest flower at such stately homes as Blenheim, Alnwick, Harewood, Chatsworth, Warwick, and Luton Hoo (among many more: at least 170 Brownian landscapes in total). Suddenly, all that fastidious, unabashedly unnatural order was swept away to be replaced by park and meadow, copse and lake, and the wonder of the ha-ha, that brilliant invisible ditch arrangement that kept the herds of cows in the park from clambering about the more formal gardens positioned near the house. In a letter dated 31 December 1782, British writer Hannah More describes her friend Mr. Brown's naturalistic methodology: "Now *there*, said he, pointing his finger, I make a comma, and there, pointing to another spot where a more decided turn is proper, I make a colon; at another part (where an interruption is desirable to break the view) a parenthesis—now a full stop, and then I begin another subject."

DO

Have one, i.e., a water feature. It doesn't matter how small or simple. For instance, for a small suburban garden, there are tons of faux lead or stone, recycling, resin wall fountains; just plop one on a wall on the exterior patio, fill the basin with water, plug it in, and bingo! You have the sound and visual delight of falling water! Ditto cast metal or stone fountains as central focal points in a garden.

Think modern. Some of the most wonderful aquatic epiphanies we have experienced as we have toured gardens are very basic. You'd be surprised by the simplicity with which these things can be achieved. A simple spout out of a square of self-draining gravel. Old millstones burbling into gravel as well. Sheets of water running from a perforated pipe down a stone or bronze wall. An oriental affair that features a bamboo pipe on a hinge that, filled via a pipe from above, tips with the weight of water running through it, and swivels to meet a second pipe that further empties into a pond. You can do this.

Figure out how to keep your recirculating water features clean, healthy, and algae-free. The most important thing is to clean the filter and cover of your pump regularly and make sure it is fully submerged when running. Constant water aeration via your pump is the best highway to cleanliness. So is a good emptying and vigororous scrubbing with bleach-enhanced water occasionally. As well, as a last resort, a bit of bleach added to the basin of a small feature will take care of the green scum at the bottom. However, if this is a bird-attracting idea: no bleach, please.

Try to be as naturalistic as possible when it comes to recirculating ponds or stream-like constructs. Think about how ponds and streams really are. Irregular of outline. Equally eccentric in terms of depth. Think of it as a real subaquatic environment over which water circulates, filled with rocks and oddities and aquatic plants. The staging of this is as important as the feature itself.

Protect your banks. If you've got a natural stream or creek running through, pay attention. This is not always easy, depending on your situation. If you, like we, are at the bottom of a steep valley sloping down to a creek, you will have your issues. When April showers start melting the snow, the erosion can be eye-opening. However testing your situation, monitor it carefully and solve the problem as immediately as possible. The longer it persists, the more difficult it will be to eliminate.

DON'T

Head to one of those preformed, free-form, obstinately flat-bottomed, hard plastic ideas that you simply pop into the ground and then do your best to disguise their patent artificiality. Gravitate instead to digging a true hole, with all its naturalistic malformations, and then line it with a stout, black, flexible, waterproof tarp. Anchor it with some landscape pins and some naturalistic-looking boulders at the edges and bottom, and the result will be far more appealing. If you are determined to have a decorative pond where there isn't one, please heed this caution, above all.

Neglect the ideas of underground piping for water features and, while you're at it, consider your irrigation system as well. These are really part of your hardscape work. Underground irrigation systems with pop-up heads need to be buried. If you covet a fountain or rill or such and have no natural water source, you will need an electric pump for recirculation. Factor these elements into your initial plan.

Put something too small in too large a space. Scale is all, as well as a thoughtful harkening back to those golden canons of yesteryear in terms of very specific geometric proportion. Do not sneeze at these ideas. There's a reason they have been honored for millennia, and it is amazing, when you achieve the right spatial relationship between objects and environments, how miraculously apparent the right relationship becomes. In short, if you have a large space, you need a large gesture.

Underestimate the upkeep of a natural water feature. As in all things garden-esque, these things can be labor intensive; you cannot choose to ignore them and let the natural order of things take its course, or you will be a blithering wreck. Silting in, falling detritus, and algae infestations are your enemy, as are runoff debris, rampant duckweed, and the occasional beaver. Still, do not be dissuaded: it's worth it.

Discount the pleasure of having such a thing, especially in a suburban and even urban environment. We lived for a long time in New York City in a house with a fountain in the courtyard behind it, with French doors and balconies we could open onto it. Can you imagine what a difference this made in urban lives defined by aural and visual assault? Not that Manhattan was anything but amazing. But to come home to the calm and the sound of that? Bliss.

5

Woodlands

Our woodlands are a typical Mid-Atlantic/Northeast hodgepodge of native trees, to which we have occasionally introduced specimens for some understory color. Elms, black walnuts, sycamores, oaks, maples, chestnuts, shagbark hickories, locusts, pines, and beeches are just some of the trees that populate our wooded areas. When we started, the understory mainly consisted of dogwoods, viburnums, and burningbush. For the most part, we elected to leave our woodlands pretty much intact, save for the ultra-necessary task of clearing out the rampant invasives (multiflora rose, grapevine, poison ivy), errant saplings, and dead wood.

The woodland north of the lake after years of clearing out invasives, errant saplings, and dead wood.

Honestly, the most we have done in the greatest part, aside from those necessities, is to enhance them with drifts of spring bulbs, particularly on the southern flank across the creek from the house, so, before the trees leaf out, shading and camouflaging those risings, we have the pretty show of splashes of yellow and white enlivening the woodland. The one largish enterprise we did embark on, however, was to clear a path within the woodland entirely surrounding the lake with a bridge over the creek at the west end. We christened this the Woodland Walk.

The Woodland Walk

Imagine, if you will, a mainly single file path, mainly of turf, announced by a pad of random flagstone and entered on the south side of the lake at the bottom of the Birch Walk, featuring mainly native woodland perennials and shrubs, spring bulbs, and specimen trees. There is a good amount of bank falling to the lake from the path around most of its circumference save for the west end, which descends to the creek and bridge we constructed to traverse to the north side of the lake. We have planted great drifts of bulbs—upward of 200,000 in total, mainly daffodils, bluebells, and grape hyacinths—on these flanks, and the early spring show, when the trees are just

This fairly virgin winter woodland at the very eastern perimeter of the farm is in need of some further invasive removal in the understory.

The spectacular scarlet of burningbush (*Euonymus alatus*) in fall is a chromatic gift to our woodland's understory.

BELOW A flag pad announces the entrance to the Woodland Walk on the south side of the lake.

beginning to unfurl, is breathtaking. Later in the season, 'Delaware Valley White' azaleas, then oakleaf hydrangeas, shrubby bottlebrush buckeyes, and magnolias take up the floriferous baton. Upslope of the path to the north and south is fairly dense woodland broken with the occasional clearing created for the purpose of revealing a garden "moment." In fact, the Woodland Walk is an excellent example of how to achieve multiple reveals and surprises as one wanders the circumference of the lake, thanks to its wooded personality.

In spring, as one enters the walk on the south side, suddenly, there's a breach in the planting to the right and left. On the right, down a grassy slope, a stone pier juts out into the lake directly across from the lake pavilion with a pair of teak benches for sunny contemplation. However, it's what's revealed on the left that's the true surprise: a set of semicircular stone steps flanked by a pair of stone columns capped with antique iron flourishes. And beyond that?

LEFT *We love grape hyacinths, particularly the deep, deep, nearly true blue flowers of Muscari armeniacum.*

RIGHT *The thousands of bulbs we have planted carpet the woodland in spring.*

BELOW RIGHT *One of several varieties of hellebores that add wonderful early spring color to the woodland.*

Bacchus rising in spring from the Bluebell Lake, surrounded by islands of peachy-pink 'Nancy of Robinhill' azaleas.

The spring show of
Spanish bluebells is followed
by a gorgeous froth of
tricyrtis in fall.

OPPOSITE TOP *The
Japanese teahouse in a sea of
hellebores and companioned
with a weeping cherry in the
heart of the woodland.*

OPPOSITE BELOW
*Various azaleas are peppered
throughout the woodland;
these pretty cultivars,
both Exbury hybrids, add
some becoming zip by the
Japanese teahouse.*

Hardy begonias are a true wonder to us, not only because of their reliable beauty but because we're so used to begonias being tender.

OPPOSITE The sizeable stone Buddha head that sits atop a tree stump near the Japanese teahouse is underplanted with ajuga, here in pretty bloom.

The truly magical sight of our greatest spring glory, the Bluebell Lake: a 70- by 40-foot oval of Spanish bluebells (*Hyacinthoides hispanica*) in the heart of the woodland boasting a few islands of peach-colored azaleas and a classically handsome statue of Bacchus hoisting his dish of wine emerging from its center. As one continues along the south side, one descends to the creek to encounter, around a bend, that fanciful twig bridge built of mountain laurel and, on the far side, the surprise of the rustic Japanese teahouse in a sea of hellebores, hardy geraniums, and ajuga, with a stone Buddha head atop a tree stump. Then, as one doubles back along the north side of the creek and lake, one enters the surprise of the Yellow & Variegated Foliage Garden.

After that, one climbs the north slope and a set of semicircular stone steps to the Counselor's Circle: an unexpectedly formal and symmetrical, stone-edged, circular turf plateau centered on that variegated dogwood with an antique iron tree bench surround. Then, as one continues along the northern path heading east, upslope to the left one encounters two more surprises nestled in the woodland: the circular Topiary Garden and, a bit farther along, in another clearing, James Fuhrman's "Akebono," underplanted with pink Spanish bluebells in spring and hardy begonias in summer. James calls his installations "contemplative spaces" and always provides a bench that complements the sculpture at hand, so that one may sit for a moment and consider it. That's a total of six surprising reveals cloistered in the woodland in a single walk around the lake.

An antique wirework bench and chairs painted a sunny yellow invite visitors to sit in the heart of the Yellow & Variegated Foliage Garden.

The Yellow & Variegated Foliage Garden

The Yellow & Variegated Foliage Garden is in the heart of the woodland on the north side of the creek and at the western end of the lake. As it was clearly in the floodplain of the creek at some

moment in time, it's a relatively flat bit of ground and fairly devoid
of any major canopy until one travels further upslope to the north.
As you might hazard to guess from its appellation, Renny's idea was
that all shrubs, trees, and perennials displayed in this garden would
sport chartreuse, striped, spotted, or light-margined leaves and yellow
blossoms, so that even on a cloudy day, it would always look like
sunlight was illuminating that secluded spot. In fact, it's as much
of a reveal and surprise as other elements along this route, as the
chroma shifts dramatically from regulation green to a far sunnier,
nearly phosphorescent idea. One might think this makes for an
overwhelmingly antic garden, with so many gregarious colors in
close proximity but, in fact, because the palette is basically green,
yellow, and white, there's a certain harmony to it all. The stars of
this garden are a golden catalpa (*Catalpa bignonioides* 'Aurea'); a
rare variegated magnolia; both a golden and a variegated maple; a
big stand of yellow wax bells (*Kirengeshoma palmata*), a wonderful

ABOVE LEFT *One of
the most remarked-upon
trees in our collection is
the quite rare Magnolia
denudata 'McCracken's
Variegated' in the Yellow
& Variegated Foliage
Garden.*

ABOVE RIGHT *The
stunning 'Forest Pansy'
redbud is a lively foil
to the variegated maple
in the foreground and
the stand of the 'Gold
Heart' bleeding heart just
behind it.*

OPPOSITE *Daffodils
carry the color theme of
the Yellow & Variegated
Foliage Garden in
early spring.*

Japanese shrub; a small grove of golden locusts as the true central feature; and a single renegade, just because: a 'Forest Pansy' redbud with its deep pink blossoms in early spring and deep purple foliage in summer. Also featured here are variegated Solomon's seal, variegated lamium, yellow iris, pale yellow-foliaged forsythia and bleeding heart, carpetings of 'Tiffindell Gold' cotula and golden creeping Jenny, and, of course, great drifts of yellow daffodils in spring. About ten years ago, we planted a pair of 'Gold Rush' dawn redwoods on the north shore of the creek. They're only about 20 feet tall at this juncture, but eventually they'll be the majestic stars of this garden.

The circular geometry of the newly conceived Topiary Garden mirrors the shape of the Pool Garden, French Garden, Mediterranean Garden, and Cutting Round.

OPPOSITE *'Gold Heart' bleeding heart is just one of the perennials that light up the Yellow & Variegated Foliage Garden in midsummer.*

The Topiary Garden

The Topiary Garden, one of the newest gardens on the farm, is really the result of a very generous bequest by a friend in Middleburg, Virginia, who decided to downsize the maintenance on her spectacular garden and rehome some of the immense clipped boxwoods she had trained and nurtured for years. Her gardeners burlap-balled them for us two falls ago, and we drove down in the big nursery truck to pick them up, seven in all, some as tall as 8 feet. Our friend has since passed on, so we are thrilled to be able to carry on a bit of her legacy here on the farm. One of the topiaries, a drum topped with a cone topped with a ball, now resides as a surprising 7-foot focal point in the Lajeski Meadow. Another is

the visual destination in a clearing in the woods behind the Urn Garden. The other five are the anchors of their very own garden: the Topiary Garden, on the north slope of the Woodland Walk. This is another circular idea, like the Mediterranean Garden. Come to think of it, the only square or rectangular "rooms" on the entire farm are the relatively small-scale Edible Rooms behind the chicken house, as our topography simply doesn't allow for much that is severely symmetrical. With all our slopes and winding paths and naturalistically planted swaths of garden, broken with the three long axes of the Birch Walk, Perennial Borders, and Pine & Dogwood Allée, circular shapes seem to us to be the obvious choice; they are more organic and, therefore, more easily integrated into our less-than-orderly whole.

The Topiary Garden is in a simple clearing in the woodland and consists of a quartet of evenly spaced, ball-capped box cones surrounding a swirling box topiary with a bird at the summit, that central feature clocking in at about 8 feet in height. We've underplanted the central topiary with white salvias and connected the four cones with a narrow circular border of false spirea. As a backdrop, we planted three eastern redbuds (*Cercis canadensis*), a birthday gift for Renny, in a semicircle on the northern edge of the cleared space, and they have just had a spectacular first flowering this season, their vibrant pinky purple so vivacious against the nascent green of the woodland. The underplantings still have a ways to go in terms of establishment, but the shape of the garden and the idea are readily apparent, and we look forward to a really glorious show in the coming years.

This wonderfully architectural box topiary provides a fitting counterpoint to the naturalistic charms of the Lajeski Meadow.

SPRING BULBS

With the exception of tulips, which we identify as being distinctly annual in nature and, therefore, not worth the effort unless you employ a slew of gardeners, spring bulbs are the most carefree and worthwhile things on earth to plant, as especially daffodils, grape hyacinths, and snowdrops are anathema to deer and will happily naturalize and spread in the bargain, giving you more bang for your buck with each passing year.

We go for the big, naturalistic gesture and find that if you simply open your bag of bulbs (they usually come in bags of 25 or so), grasp it by the bottom, and swing it round, allowing the bulbs to fall where they may, you end up with an arrangement that appears as if Mother Nature had cast them there herself. Short of that, don't plant them like little soldiers but in free-form drifts and clouds, spacing them 4 to 6 inches apart. Also, we've

✤ *These enchanting Narcissus 'Tête-à-tête' and other daffodils carpet the lawn along the north side of the creek in spring.*

learned that adding a bit of bone meal to the soil or to the bottom of each hole will give your bulbs an extra boost. When we first started planting, we nearly maimed ourselves by employing a handheld bulb planter, the type that plants a single bulb— you take it by the handle and jam the sharpened edge into the ground and then remove the plug of earth you've captured. If you are planting just a few bulbs, this is doable. If you have ordered several thousand, you are at risk of damaging your wrists and shoulders for life. Some years in, we hit upon the idea of rototilling great cloud forms and popping in the bulbs, maybe 50 per cloud, about 4 inches deep (the rule of thumb is twice as deep as the size of the bulb, pointy end up), until we discovered the winning merits of a sizeable auger attached to a power drill, which, while back to a one-at-a-time idea, still lets the machine do most of the work and also allows you to plant among the roots of trees, which is an auspicious site indeed for most bulbs. Some of our favorite spring bulbs on the farm:

» *Allium bulgaricum*

» *Allium* 'Mount Everest'

» *Allium* 'Globemaster'

» *Allium karataviense*

» *Allium caeruleum*

» *Allium* 'Pinball Wizard'

» *Bellevalia paradoxa*

» *Camassia* 'Blue Melody'

» *Camassia cusickii*

» *Chionodoxa* 'Pink Giant'

» *Muscari armeniacum*

» *Muscari armeniacum* 'Valerie Finnis'

» *Narcissus* 'Sinopel'

» *Narcissus* 'Ice Folly'

» *Narcissus* 'Lemon Beauty'

» *Narcissus* 'Mondragon'

» *Narcissus* 'Passionale'

» *Narcissus* 'Acropolis'

» *Narcissus* 'Angel Eyes'

» *Narcissus* 'Pink Angel'

» *Narcissus* 'Fragrant Breeze'

» *Narcissus* 'Sorbet'

» *Narcissus* 'Limbo'

» *Narcissus* 'Love Call'

» *Narcissus* 'Sun Disc'

» *Narcissus* 'Velasquez'

» *Narcissus* 'Border Beauty'

» *Narcissus* 'Decoy'

» *Narcissus* 'Falconet'

» *Narcissus* 'Petit Four'

» *Narcissus* 'Silent Valley'

» *Narcissus* 'Princess Zaide'

*While many applauded the rise of the naturalistic, others lamented
the loss of the overwrought and hyper-refined, as in this example
at the Prague Castle Gardens in the Czech Republic.*

Classical
LAMENTATION

While many factions were avid supporters of the purposeful return to the "natural" in garden theory, sending parterres and avenues and ostentatious hardscape tumbling, others lamented Capability Brown's sweeping away of artificiality. And, certainly, this new British vogue for the Arcadian and picturesque was met with huge suspicion, not only in those countries that had birthed the rigorous human manipulation of the landscape but also by a good coterie of local Anglo denizens of taste. The English poet William Cowper, writing to one Lady Hesketh in 1788, keenly lamented "the things which our modern improvers of parks and pleasure grounds have displaced without mercy; because, forsooth, they are rectilinear. It is a wonder they do not quarrel with the sunbeams for the same reason." In 1828, Sir Walter Scott took Brownian landscape to task as having "no more resemblance to that nature which we desire to see imitated, than the rouge of an antiquated coquette, having all the marks of a sedulous toilet, bears to the artless blush of a cottage girl." Even Gertrude Jekyll, whom we always imagined would be a great Brownian champion, wrote of him in 1896: "Everything was to be 'natural'—sham natural generally—and especially there was to be water everywhere." And in *The Education of a Gardener* (1962), British garden designer Russell Page chastised Brown for "encouraging his wealthy clients to tear out their splendid formal gardens and replace them with his facile compositions of grass, tree clumps, and rather shapeless pools and lakes."

DO

Put forestry maintenance at the top of your list if you have a good amount of wooded acreage. It is imperative that you remove dead wood before it topples, saplings that are encroaching on mature trees, and whatever invasives may be roiling through the understory. Of particular importance is the removal of dead wood: the last thing you need is for some massive limb to come crashing down on you or your house. And this is not a one-time-only idea. Do be vigilant, or you will unleash the Leviathan.

Turn to native and naturalizing plants as a logical place to start your woodland planting. They will not only acclimatize instantly but, in the long run, be as relatively carefree as possible. The best part, of course, is that the naturalizers will increase in number over time, not only enlarging their coverage but making themselves available for division to decorate another area of your property. This is another "visit your local nursery for inspiration" idea.

Scroll a few strolling paths through your woodland. It's perfectly pleasant to wander freely through a forest, but it's a lovelier idea to follow a sinuous lane of bark or pine needles through a glorious green canopy of mature trees (the redwood forests in northern California, for instance) banked with a few azaleas or rhododendrons, this allowing you enough visual distance to see the forest *and* the trees.

Consider drifts of groundcovers or bulbs in the understory to add some ameliorating color to the forest floor, which will mainly be leaf-mulch brown. Again, choose the right ones (daffodils, grape hyacinths, bluebells, lamium, pachysandra, vinca) and they will naturalize, providing a constantly spreading carpet of color.

Plant the occasional small-statured flowering tree to enliven the understory. Our native dogwoods and viburnums are dazzling in late spring. Redbuds are wonderful because they flower before leafing out, right on the dark wood, so the color is incredibly intense. Magnolias are irreplaceable for spectacular blossom, as are flowering quince, crabapples, and cherries. In general, spring-flowering ideas are probably your best bet as, once the forest canopy greens in, sunlight (or lack thereof) will be an issue.

DON'T

Mistake your woodland for a non-garden. By culling the trees to the best specimens and removing dead matter and invasives, thereby increasing air flow and light, and then creating mid- and understory interest with smaller trees, shrubs, and groundcovers, you can turn a woodland into the most romantic garden spot on earth, especially in the heat of summer when some green, cooling shade is just the ticket.

Hesitate to create a living room moment in the heart of the woodland, even if it's just some log benches and a stone fire pit. There is something magical about coming to a clearing in the woods outfitted for a cozy get-together or even a picnic lunch or dinner. If you do have a fire pit, make sure, just like in camping, you have the means to make *absolutely sure* it is out, with the coals scattered, before you leave.

Waste all that downed and culled timber that is lying about. Rent a log splitter or chipper and supply yourself with split logs for your winter fires or chipped bark for the paths you'll be creating in your woodland. They are surprisingly easy to use and will spin chaff into gold. *Don't* forget to wear safety goggles during these employs.

Fail to add focal points to the woodland. A clearing and seating idea is one thing. But so is a bit of surprising sculpture or piece of topiary or a secret grove of understory trees or a single spectacular magnolia or even a little orchard sequestered in the woodland. A bit of reveal and surprise never hurts.

Ever forget that you are preserving and maybe even enhancing a habitat for birds and woodland creatures on your property, a place in which they can flourish in the face of lost habitats everywhere one looks. You are doing something wonderful for all our earthly brethren but also for our planet, as with the encroachment of civilization, these saved green spaces are what will be our salvation, if there is to be one. The jury's still out.

6

Open *Spaces*

*Our rescue horses,
enjoying their own
dedicated paddock.*

With so much woodland and then mainly lawn interconnecting the gardens at the heart of the farm, it's easy to overlook the open spaces that are neither one nor the other, i.e., the meadows, pastures, and naked flanks that are a rich part of our farm environment. With the exception of the Dell, they hover on the edges of the property, either up by Thompson Mill Road on the south side or up beyond the pool to the north and east. We have established loosely composed gardens in some of these areas, in all cases erring on the side of the naturalistic. However, we still have what the Warner/Thompson family surely had: paddocks and pastures, theirs for their dairy herds and ours for our horses, sheep, and goats.

*We have real open
spaces (pastures and
meadows) that are truly
naked to the sun,
and then partially open
spaces like this one,
dotted with native trees.*

The sheep and goats feed in a paddock as well as the former riding
ring attached to the upper barn and viewed to the north side of the
Perennial Borders. The horses, stabled in the lower barn, are in the
paddock on the south side of the Perennial Borders, which allows
them to ford Fire Creek and access the front pasture, which extends
all the way to Thompson Mill Road. That these areas have remained
true to their historic uses is, to us, what makes Hortulus Farm
distinctive from other public gardens. We are a farm as well as
a garden.

The Peony Ribbon

The Peony Ribbon cuts a sinuous swath up near Thompson Mill
Road, linking the nursery operation to our driveway. Much like our
Perennial Borders, the scheme involves two broad borders flanking
a substantial greensward, snaking their way, east to west, across what
was formerly a cornfield, let to a neighboring farmer. We planted
about 3,000 peonies in the two borders 30 years ago with the
intention of employing them as a spring crop and selling them in
12-stem bundles to the flower markets in New York and Philadelphia.
Renny, of course, because of his event and flower business, was very
familiar to all the wholesale purveyors at the market in New York,
and his reputation seemed to have infiltrated south to Philadelphia as

*Our sheep and goats
are housed on the lower
level of the upper barn
(see the sheep standing
in the doorway?) and
pastured to the east
and north of it.*

*Perhaps our favorite
of the four lactiflora
peonies we cultivate,
'Sarah Bernhardt',
with surely as much
beauty and drama as
its namesake.*

well. The borders shift in color from the deep red/burgundy of 'Karl
Rosenfield', who introduced this cultivar in 1908, at the nursery
end, through the luscious pink of 'Sarah Bernhardt' (Lemoine 1906),
to the virginal glory (with intermittent dashes of red) of 'Festiva
Maxima' (Mielles 1851), and, finally, near the drive, the single pink,
golden-stamened 'Sea Shell' (Sass 1937), winner of the American
Peony Society gold medal in 1990.

To say they are a stunning sight in peak season is an
understatement: there are literally thousands of blooms in great drifts
of color, one transitioning softly into the next as they meander across
the field. We had backed the borders with hydrangeas accented with

the occasional crepe myrtle, but the crepe myrtles seem to have all but expired over the past two winters, although there is some new growth sprouting from their roots. Admittedly, crepe myrtles are a bit dicey this far north, but they'd put on a good show for ten years or so; the jury's still out on whether they will be removed or not. We've also elected not to crop the peonies for the past couple of years. In the years we did cut them for the markets, as you can imagine, we were left with a pretty spotty show on site. Also, prepping them for market is a very labor-intensive exercise, as each stem needs to have the auxiliary buds removed, leaving only the central blossom, so as to have the largest, sturdiest flower. And, finally, the margins, what with the labor involved to debud, cut, pack, and transport them to market, became nearly negligible. Perhaps we'll return to cropping them but, for the time being, it's awfully nice to have the full show on display at the end of May. Sadly, the peony season is famously short—three weeks in a good year—which, in part, is why they are so cherished when they decide to unfurl themselves, so we should all enjoy what are surely the most extravagant and fragrant of flowers while we may.

An early morning mist rises to reveal the dramatic sweep of the Peony Ribbon scrolling across an upper field on Thompson Mill Road.

The Lajeski Meadow

The Lajeski Meadow is in the farthest northeast corner of the farm on the last parcel of land we acquired, preserved by and fittingly named for our friend and advisory board chairman Glen Lajeski. It is accessed from the top of the Pine & Dogwood Allée, from the Mediterranean Garden, and from the Specimen Arboretum. Of all our gardens, it is by far the most naturalistic idea as, while we have helped it along with the occasional perennial introduction of this and that, it is basically a native meadow into which we have mown a few paths leading to the other gardens on that far eastern perimeter. Some of the plants native to meadows in our zone 6b are butterfly weed, cow parsley, various rudbeckias and echinaceas, lupines, oxeye daisies, coreopsis, cinquefoil, the tiny white native asters that frost the fields in autumn, and, of course, several native grasses, like big bluestem, little bluestem, switchgrass, and wild ryes. To this mix we have popped in swaths of common blue wood aster and false

The common blue wood aster adds wonderful color to the Lajeski Meadow in early fall.

OPPOSITE TOP *We have enhanced our native meadow with the occasional stand of perennials or grasses and now simply mow paths in it in season.*

OPPOSITE BELOW *While not the Crayola-hued meadow of everyone's dreams, a native meadow can have a subtler charm all its own.*

sunflower as well as some big stands of grasses. We mow the entire meadow once in early spring, then let it grow through the season, mowing only the paths through it for the duration.

From the top of the Lajeski Meadow, one has an impressive territorial view of the pastoral Windybush Valley as well as the beautiful dressage facility we're lucky enough to have next door with their horses grazing in their paddocks. Honestly, with its extensive vista and nearly native demeanor, it's a lovely, restful change from the more cloistered and intensive plantings of the rest of the gardens. We've placed two notable focal points up there: that massive box topiary of a cone sitting on a drum capped by a ball, adopted from Virginia, and an even larger, zany piece of sculpture donated by a neighbor in Yardley. He somehow ended up with it in his garage and believes it was created by students at Princeton University to represent some molecular structure or other. It was delivered in several sections but, when assembled, it proved to be a hulking

The winter view looking east from the Urn Garden across the Lajeski Meadow, its focal-point topiary dusted with snow.

OPPOSITE *An oversized bronze apple embellishes the old crabapple we unearthed beneath a mountain of invasives in the lower meadow.*

stainless steel creature with six legs and an arched back painted with bands of yellow and white. We think it looks quite marvelous and certainly surprising when chanced upon in that great open space.

When we acquired this parcel, further down the Lajeski Meadow on the east side of the Mediterranean Garden, we uncovered what is probably a 150-year-old crabapple under a mountain of poison ivy, bittersweet, multiflora rose, and other vining invasives so inpenetrable, one could not even tell there was a tree beneath it. It's a magnificent tree—we're so lucky to have saved it, and we've cheekily placed an enormous bronze apple, 2 feet in circumference, at its feet. We tell our tours we're always amazed at the size of the fruit it drops. Thankfully, they laugh. And, finally, we placed the Chinese moon window that was another birthday present for Renny many years ago (a huge octagonal frame on legs forged by our farm manager out of steel I-beams) on the property line there, overlooking the Windybush Valley, the enchanting philosophy behind a "moon" window being that, as one moves past it, the Arcadian picture in the frame changes.

This creature-like molecular sculpture, donated by a neighbor, creates what can only be termed a "surprise" at the top of the Lajeski Meadow.

OPPOSITE *This now-rusted steel Chinese moon window was built by our farm manager, Bob Ritchie, as a birthday gift to Renny.*

The Specimen Aboretum

The Specimen Arboretum, an idea that was hatched more out of a
sense of necessity than true horticultural inspiration, was another
joint effort with our friend Glen, who preserved this land as well.
In fact, he still visits the farm, traveling from his olive orchard in
Sonoma, to help plant and tend this particular patch. It is accessed
from behind the Pool Garden through a large pair of decorative iron
gates we purchased at the New York Botanical Garden's antiques
show, now situated between two of the immense American hollies
that ring the pool plateau on direct axis with the Perennial Borders.
As inveterate plant collectors, always enthusiastically hunting down
the latest, the rarest, and the most unusual cultivars appropriate to our
zone 6b, we have ended up with more than a few one-off "trophies,"
and the question was where on earth (or on the farm) would they be
displayed to best advantage? Thus was born the Specimen Arboretum:
a kind of gallery of interesting cultivars, with the unifying element
being a partiality to conifers and Japanese maples. The area in back of
the pool had always had a few sparse stands of trees, so we decided to
corral them into a series of island beds, finally adding a central bed
that featured a golden catalpa and a splendid frostproof Lunaform pot.

Conifers displayed in the Specimen Arboretum include junipers
and firs, white and mugo pines, cedar of Lebanon, and blue, Norway,
and oriental spruce. The Japanese maple cultivars we showcase include
both palmate and cut- or lace-leaf varieties like 'Aconitifolium',
'Shishigashira', 'Crimson Queen', and 'Bloodgood', and it is the
interplay between the blues and greens of the conifers and the reds
and golds of the maples that were of interest to us. Then there are the
host of one-offs, like a handsome English oak, 'Summer Chocolate'
mimosa, a ginkgo, and a truly unusual dogwood (*Cornus sanguinea*
'Compressa'), all these underplanted with an assortment of hostas,
low-growing perennials and grasses, and groundcovers like 'Wolong
Ghost' euonymus, 'Max Frei' and 'Ingwersen's Variety' geraniums,
'Iron Butterfly' ironweed, and 'Angelina' sedum. Also, if you look very
carefully, in the central bed surrounding the catalpa, there are three

TOP *Whatever the
season, decorative iron
gates and a Lunaform
pot add to the Specimen
Arboretum scene.*

BELOW LEFT *This
white pine is one of
the many conifers that
provide interesting color
and textural contrast
to the other specimens
in the arboretum.*

BELOW RIGHT *The
sun illuminating the
beautifully cut leaves of
a Japanese maple as
they color up in spring.*

Two of the Japanese maple cultivars that lend a thematic cohesiveness to the Specimen Arboretum.

stones like the ones we have employed up in the Temple Canum. Pamm, Glen's old and dear friend from the dog show circuit who lived just across the river, left us way too early, succumbing to bone cancer after a long and valiant battle. In her final months, when she was having difficulty walking, she would drive over in her yellow VW Bug with the vase of flowers attached to the dashboard and a *Carpe diem!* bumper sticker; we would lend her a golf cart, and she would ride around the farm, running Shane, her beautiful, blue-eyed Australian cattle dog, and having some time with nature. When she died, we were happy to keep some of her ashes with us and offered to adopt Shane but, ultimately, he went to another friend. However, when he finally passed away, his ashes were returned to us to be buried beside Pamm. We know the farm was one of their favorite places on earth, and we're very happy to have them reunited with us now. Glen's mother, Estelle, who died in her 90s at a nearby nursing facility, also has some of her ashes buried there, topped with a stone. May they all rest in peace, and rest assured: Renny and I will be very happy up on the hill with our dogs when our time comes.

Our friend Pamm was one of the farm's greatest champions, and we are thrilled we could reunite some of her ashes with those of Shane, her beloved dog, when his time came.

The Dell

The amazing Scandinavian influence in garden design—championing a wild, meadow-y, almost free-form yet gorgeously effective style of great drifts and ribbons of sustainable planting with an emphasis on grasses, hardy perennials, and self-seeders—has taken the horticultural world by storm, and we are totally in love with it, as witnessed in our newest garden effort, the Dell, our largest-ever project on the farm. Following the assault of Hurricane Sandy, we lost upward of two dozen immense trees on the slope above the lake. This had been fairly dense woodland, and we must have had a severe wind shear cut through because the trees toppled like dominoes, one hitting the next and taking its neighbor down as it fell. It took us nearly two years of chainsawing and chipping to clean up the resultant mess, leaving that bank nearly denuded. We had had some vague thoughts of opening up the area slightly and doing some drifts of shrub and

bulb planting, but now we had what practically amounted to a large blank slate. And, as every diehard gardener ultimately feels in his or her heart, loss is easily turned to fresh opportunity with the correct mindset.

And so the Dell was conceived with that dreamy, drift-y Nordic vision in mind. To date, we've planted 1,500 azaleas, 1,500 hydrangeas, and 2,000 perennials (including hardy hibiscus and geraniums, 'Caesar's Brother' Siberian iris, Russian sage, and various grasses and hostas) in great drifts on that northern flank, with a new series of chipped paths etching their way through, leading to the equally nascent topiary and sculpture gardens on the north side of the Woodland Walk. We have had parts of a gothic folly, brought back from England, in the upper barn for many years now and have a thought that we may erect it at the top of the Dell's slope as an ultimate destination. A subsidiary runoff stream cuts through the Dell

Great drifts of golden ragwort (Packera aurea) and other perennials carpet the partially wooded flanks of the new garden in the Dell.

OPPOSITE *A painted wire art ball sits atop one of the stumps left by Hurricane Sandy in the Dell.*

MEADOW PLANTING

The plain truth is, like swimming pools, everyone wants a meadow but only a dedicated few will have a successful one. It's always amusing for us to hear people of one's acquaintance start their actualization of a meadow idea by declaring, "We're just going to let it go to meadow"—as if, with a *Bewitched* twitch of their nose, they will be rewarded with poppies, lupines, rudbeckias, asters, and oxeye daisies decorating their fields as far as the eye can see. Nothing could be further from the truth as, in fact, the institution of a successful flowering meadow idea is one of the most difficult garden conceits imaginable. In a nutshell, unless you try to institute your meadow in one of two ways, whatever is in your meadow natively will eventually choke out your additions, and the plot will entirely revert to native meadow. Of course, if you are lucky, your native meadow might be pretty enough on its own. However, if you want the children's storybook version, all reds and blues and yellows and whites dotting grassy fields, you will accomplish it thusly: Either—1. Plow and sow annually; this means cutting the meadow in early spring, tilling what's left under, and reseeding the entire meadow with a flowering meadow mix, that year and every one thereafter. Or—2. You can call our friend Larry Weaner, the "Meadow King," who has made a science of how to establish a flowering meadow

Anyone who thinks one has only to cast some seeds upon the ground to achieve a meadow is in for a surprise. (Design by Larry Weaner)

using a three-year process. In order to achieve long-term sustainability and low maintenance, the plants must be, almost without exception, native to your particular region as well as truly perennial: most commercially available meadow mixes go for the immediate bang and are composed of a good number of annuals and biennials. After the initial seeding of perennial cultivars, Larry recommends allowing the introduced plant matter to grow beneath the native invasives by mowing the meadow to 4 to 6 inches the first year. In the second year, when the introduced perennials have gotten a toehold, spot weeding, herbicide application to the invasives, or cutting the meadow again just before the most prominent invasives seed will be of the essence. By the third year, your meadow should be sufficiently established and will need limited control of invasives moving forward.

on the eastern perimeter, and over it we have built a stone bridge, which allows one to climb the steep slope to the east, flanked by a pair of life-size Beaux-Arts American Indians sporting vaguely Grecian togas, to achieve the French Garden at the summit. The Dell still needs a bit of maturing to reach its full potential, but the bones are there and, as the years roll on, it is sure to become one of our most notable gestures.

✠   *The Victorian bedding scheme, with its garishly themed carpets of violently hued annuals, thankfully met a merciful demise.*

TASTE
Takes a Holiday

Now, as we approach the mid to late 19th century, we chance upon what was, surely, a significant low point in the history of garden design: the nightmare of the Victorian bedding scheme. It was almost as if artificiality, kicked to the curb by the new taste for the picturesque and naturalistic, had rallied its forces for one final, hideous onslaught on garden style in the form of mounded parterre beds filled with the most intricately styled and garishly hued annual plantings imaginable, often topped with cockades of equally repugnant orange cannas or purple caladiums. One can still visit this moment of horticultural aberrance at Waddesdon Manor in England, that great Victorian Rothschild ode to a surfeit of silver, flocked wallpaper, Sèvres china, and oversized gilt furniture larger than one imagined possible. There the garden beds stay rebelliously true to the era of the house's construction (1874 to 1885), with a rather paint-by-numbers or needlepoint-canvas look about them, as the planting scheme is really about "painting" with specifically colored plant matter to achieve a precise, very intensive, nearly wallpaper-like design. The blue of succulents or ageratum, the red of crimson-foliaged begonias, and the acid yellow and oranges of marigolds, for instance, so not part of the British garden lexicon, were bandied about with abandon. In 1881, the great William Robinson, who was to rescue horticulture from this dark moment, sounded its death knell: "Its highest results need hardly be described; they are seen in all our great public gardens; our London and many other city parks show them in the shape of beds filled with vast quantities of flowers, covering the ground frequently in a showy way. . . . I will not here enter into the question of the merits of this system; it is enough to state that even on its votaries it is beginning to pall."

DO

Try leaving a field you usually mow (if you have one as part of your acreage) uncut for a season and see what transpires. Inevitably, the local thugs (mainly grasses) will rule the roost in that particular plot, choking out the less hearty and perhaps more decorative inhabitants, but that doesn't mean there won't be plants of ornamental interest in the tough native mix. Give it a try: while it may not result in the color-studded meadow of your dreams, it may have a subtler "amber waves of grain" charm all its own and will surely save you mowing time.

Consider, if you have a surfeit of open space and a rural context, letting some portion of your fields to a local farmer for the production of corn or soy or rye. All these are very appealing in a field—the soy a nice blue/green note, rye grass with its feathery plumes, corn as pleasingly stalwart and high, of course, as an elephant's eye. These not only enhance that truly rural feeling and are good for a whole lot of reasons for a whole lot of people, but letting your land should also put a tidy sum in your bank account and may even lower your taxes by giving you a farmstead designation.

Create a visual destination and garden "moment" in an open space. We suppose this is basically a focal-point idea, although this is a notion that can take on many personalities. An interesting piece of sculpture like the molecular creature that inhabits our meadow. A twig or woven willow construct like the ones created by American artist Patrick Dougherty. A single gargantuan specimen tree like our old crabapple. Or, much like the woodland notion, a mown space with a surprise seating area overlooking a view. *Not* a Victorian bedding scheme.

Think about banking open spaces where they meet woodland with the classic idea of "transitional woodland," i.e., a kind of loose border composed of copses of small ornamental trees and shrubs, and perhaps some groundcover. For instance, birches, azaleas and other rhododendrons, and vinca or pachysandra. Planted in a fairly naturalistic fashion, they both soften and beautify what could be a decidedly abrupt horticultural transition.

Embrace the idea of a "gallery" of notable specimen plants, either placing them in a border or unifying them in a themed garden. The Yellow & Variegated Foliage Garden is a good example of a scheme in which foliage color unites a large number of one-off specimens in a garden moment. The Specimen Arboretum unifies its island beds and singular shrubs and trees with the repetitive theme of Japanese maples and conifers.

DON'T

Feel the need to fill every open space. Every eye needs a rest if it is to absorb more information, particularly of the intricate intensity common to most gardens of a classical conceit. One of our favorite things about the English countryside is the wealth of open fields given to grazing sheep or herds of cattle or simply left to display their acres of acid-yellow rape or crimson poppies. There is something so soothing about such open spaces, especially when juxtaposed with the walled and terraced and bordered complexities of the typical stately home.

Hesitate to contemplate the addition of a pond or lake in the midst of an open space, if it is in your purview and budget. Such water features are especially successful in open spaces; not only do they create a focal point, but they also brilliantly reflect the sun and sky and provide admirable drinking spots for local wildlife. Surround them with a willow or two and some cattails or stands of substantial grasses, and you will have transformed a blank space into one of enchantment as well as a wonderful source of refreshment for a whole host of our earthly brethren.

Scoff at the idea of a maze. One sees them all the time around Halloween, mown into fields and meadows, as a source of holiday amusement, generally involving marshmallow roasting, pumpkin carving, and mulled cider. Lift this idea out of that moment and contemplate it as a seasonal garden attraction in your open space. They're awfully easy to implement, wonderful to view from on high, and can turn a blah space into a truly interesting one in a thrice.

Refuse to entertain the idea of introducing a few copses into your open space. These aboreal ideas not only add scale and vertical and spatial interest to a blank slate but, with the right choices, trees can also add wonderful pops of color and texture. Think golden and purple foliage, for instance, as well as fall color to enliven what would otherwise be a large field of green sameness.

Eschew the idea of bringing something living and beneficial in. Sheep. A few cows. Beehives. Bluebird houses. Any of these will bring both life and love of your natural brethren into your space. Yes, sheep and cattle need a shelter, feeding, and some looking after. As do bee colonies. Bluebird houses are pretty much maintenance-free. You will be amazed by how much this life adds to yours. The benefit is immeasurable.

7

Palette
& Planting

One of the most important considerations Renny put on the table when we began our public garden adventure was the principle that we would be a source of horticultural education and inspiration for the people who visited. Paramount in this notion was the idea that each of the gardens we created would offer a plant palette and personality that were distinctly different from those of the others, so that as one wandered the farm, one would experience many different cultural styles and planting combinations, particularly vignettes featuring unfamiliar and unusual specimens: none of this "native and sustainable plants only" manifesto for us. If it will work in our zone 6b and we like the looks of it, we say what's not to love?

Of course, in siting all our horticultural choices, we would have to give a nod to the specifics of their cultural requirements. Did they want sun or shade? Dry or wet? Sandy, clayey, or nicely loamy? A pH kind to blueberries and rhododendrons, or not?

In the beginning, we started small, taking on what we imagined would be an intimate, very manageable first project: the tiny turf forecourt between house and drive, circumscribed by that barrier of ancient boxwoods. We envisioned a charming, cottagey English perennial idea—loose and country-appropriate—flanking a path to the front door, but wherever we put shovel to ground, we hit stone. A good number of stones. Finally, rather than cutting down into the turf, we scraped at it horizontally with the shovel and, under 6 inches of sod, unearthed a long-forgotten stone patio. It transpired, however, that the massive, rough-hewn pavers, some a yard square or greater, were sufficiently spaced to allow us to plant in between. So, being adaptable as all gardeners must learn to be when faced with not perhaps an insurmountable obstacle but one which,

Two classical arcades grown with wisteria flank the native dogwood in the center of the Temple Canum in this particular garden moment.

OPPOSITE
'Mount Everest' allium, sweetpeas, lady's mantle, bachelor's buttons, 'Taplow Blue' globe thistle, and 'Buckland' astrantia, are just a few of the perennial stalwarts displayed at Hortulus Farm.

however unexpected, proved to have merits of its own, we changed
direction and instituted instead a very spontaneous, green planting
with pops of tiny white and blue blossom: Japanese painted fern and
others, club moss, miniature hostas, Solomon's seal, trilliums, star of
Bethlehem, 'Valerie Finnis' grape hyacinth, the enchanting green-
eyed 'Sinopel' daffodil, and true-blue forget-me-nots. In a way, the
juxtaposition of all those greens, whites, and blues with the craggy,
rain-slicked grays and browns of the native stone of both forecourt
and house manages to be both cottagey and woodsy, which, to us,
is an extremely "farm appropriate" idea. And that's basically how
we proceeded as new horticultural moments and gestures presented
themselves to us.

The Perennial Borders

The Perennial Borders were certainly our most intensive planting idea on the farm, as they're quite long, quite broad, and need to bloom successively all summer. Also, since we have populated them with crabapples, cherries, and midsize shrubs (mallows, spireas), there are pockets of both shade and sun. With the exception of the recently introduced dahlias, all plants are perennial, flowering in a soft palette of white, blue, pink, and purple, and the list is long. We always plant in odd-numbered groupings of five or seven or nine to create asymmetrical masses of color, clearly with some attention to height and hue; but mainly our borders are quite blowsy and spontaneous in feeling, one thing drifting into another, with the crabs and cherries providing great clouds of pink overhead in spring when the perennials are just poking their noses up.

The quiet Perennial Borders in early spring, when things are just starting to come alive.

The Perennial Borders in late summer, with 'Autumn Joy' sedum, phlox, and turtleheads leading the fray.

ABOVE *The crabapples and cherries light up the Perennial Borders in a quite spectacular fashion each spring.*

We also encourage some foliage bang-for-the buck, for instance, in the silver-gray of lamb's ear and artemisia and the deep purple of self-seeding perilla. The borders then bloom in their soft pastel palette all season long, the earliest flush being composed of bachelor's buttons, hardy geraniums, alliums, and miniature iris. Soon lamiums, fairy roses, salvias, lady's mantle, hardy begonias, and columbines chime in, followed later in the season by, among others, tiarellas, brunneras, echinops, dianthus, anemones, heucheras, daisies, lythrum, phlox, and Joe Pye weed. And then, just when you think the curtain is about to close on the blooming season, the 'Autumn Joy' sedums and dahlias in shades of white, pink, and purple really dazzle in August and September. Maintenance-wise, we cut down the borders in earliest spring, weed and mulch, and crisp up their leading edges. Then, through the season, we do a bit of staking and certainly some deadheading but, otherwise, we simply let the borders do their freewheeling thing, as we think this less structured idea is better suited to our farm vernacular than a prim, strictly organized, strictly perennial, strictly Anglo idea.

BELOW LEFT
Culver's root and phlox create wonderful textural and chromatic contrast in the Perennial Borders.

BELOW RIGHT *Joe Pye weed (Eupatorium purpureum) is one of those great garden brutes that, nearly weed-like, shrug off harsh, unsympathetic conditions with nary a sigh.*

'Zagreb' tickseed makes a nearly phosphorescent edging statement in the front row of these emphatically extroverted borders.

The Summer Borders

The Summer Borders are borders of a decidedly different personality. First of all, they are built on that steep, concave crescent standing naked to the sun and serving as the northern perimeter of the Pool Garden, so that, in effect, the entire garden is dramatically raked like a theatrical stage, which really puts its inhabitants on display. Secondly, trees and shrubs are a huge part of this planting and the palette is dramatically different from the subtle hues of the Perennial Borders. In an almost tropical celebration of the heat and swelter of high summer, here our color notes are full-on gregarious. Envision if you will an anything-but-demure blossom palette of reds, yellows, and oranges—trumpet and daylilies, oxeye daisies, helenium, and 'Zagreb' tickseed to mention a few color-keyed choices—all coming into brilliant bloom midsummer. A trio of weeping copper beeches and several franklinias, among other trees, anchor the back of each of these borders, with smokebushes, staghorn sumac, and barberries

The Summer Borders on the north side of the pool plateau combine perennials with major trees like weeping copper beech and shrubs like smokebush, barberry, and bottlebrush buckeye.

OPPOSITE LEFT
A weeping copper beech in the Summer Borders, here showing its lovely spring color.

OPPOSITE RIGHT
One of the most vibrant contributors to the yellow/red/orange blossom palette of these borders is 'Lucifer' crocosmia: could there be a more gregarious scarlet?

in the shrubby mid-range. Perennially, plume poppy and helianthus are the tall boys in the back row; lilies, variegated giant reed, and kniphofias populate the mid-range, with brilliant scarlet crocosmia and patches of dwarf 'Whitestripe' bamboo contributing to the front row. We have also added a dash of white in the vanilla-colored panicles of bottlebrush buckeyes, the blossom of the franklinias, and the twin stands of oxeye daisy, as there's nothing like white bloom to set off more colorful neighbors. To say these borders are vivacious at their height would be an understatement.

The Woodland Walk

The Woodland Walk is surely our most colorful spring idea, with its great drifts of naturalizing daffodils, Spanish bluebells, squill, snowdrops, and grape hyacinths, but it is also one of our more naturalistic gestures, filled with mainly native and naturalizing plants, these sited to appear as if they were born there. As well, as we began our gardening adventure, we were lucky enough to be the recipients of a number of bequests from Renny's business in New York. Among these, we happily inherited 300 balled 'Delaware Valley White' azaleas that had banked the entrance to Carnegie Hall for its 90th anniversary celebration in 1981. So, much like their initial application, Renny decided we would use them to bank the entrance to the walk with a flurry of white in spring.

Native and other perennial plantings include drifts of both Canadian and oriental ginger, Jack-in-the-pulpit, twinleaf, dame's rocket, trilliums, pulmonarias, pachysandra, 'Moonlight' Japanese hydrangea vine, and the marvel of the Bluebell Lake on the southern slope above the path, not to mention the many varieties of specimen magnolias that ring the lake. At the start of this enterprise, we visited local nurseries to get a feel for what natives were available and suitable for planting in our zone 6b, but we soon widened our search to include non-native varieties that piqued our interest. Chief among these was Renny's growing obsession with magnolias: to date, we have planted about 20 different sorts, including *Magnolia grandiflora*,

In late May, one is nearly cocooned on the south side of the Woodland Walk, with native dogwoods and pale pink azaleas joining in with the Delaware Valley Whites to put on a fairytale-like display.

Magnolia kobus and the hybrids 'Judy Zuk', 'Betty', and 'Ann' are just some of the magnolias that ring the lake.

OPPOSITE *With so many woodland plants blooming successively, there's always something of interest to see during the garden season.*

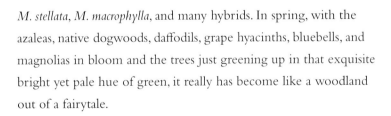

M. stellata, *M. macrophylla*, and many hybrids. In spring, with the azaleas, native dogwoods, daffodils, grape hyacinths, bluebells, and magnolias in bloom and the trees just greening up in that exquisite bright yet pale hue of green, it really has become like a woodland out of a fairytale.

The super-sized
leaves of *Magnolia
macrophylla* appear
to have been cast to
the ground by a giant
each fall.

OPPOSITE
*A magnolia enjoys
its reflection in
early spring.*

The Terrace Garden

We will end this chapter with the reminder that not all gardens need to be in the ground. As we have mentioned, we added a double terrace below the house overlooking Fire Creek, the lower terrace centered on that koi pond with the salvaged stone coping. The upper terrace has two planting pockets flanking the stairs to the lawn, these planted with hydrangeas, tree peonies, and cotoneaster. Flanking both sets of steps to the lawn, the lower wall of the terraces is planted with deep beds of shrub roses (and more tree peonies and cotoneaster). Additionally, there are lead Versailles boxes arranged in pairs flanking the stairs leading to the lower terrace, each containing one leg of antique wirework arcades grown with honeysuckle and roses. Aside from those elements, every other plant on the terraces comes potted out of the greenhouses in spring and summers, as a kind of display garden of tender plants: clustered on the ground, arrayed on a series of tables, and gushing from an antique iron plant stand that is the

In August, the immense 'Tardiva' hydrangeas flanking the steps to the lawn on the upper terrace burst into bloom.

OPPOSITE *That's a night-blooming cereus in the foreground and a variegated solanum lollipop standard in the Versailles box, underplanted with blue plumbago.*

Even in early spring, when it's still too early to bring out tender plants, the terraces are a lovely place to catch a ray of sun.

ANNUALS?

When we think of annuals, in general, we think of those garishly hued marigolds and begonias and ageratums one spies at the entrance to home developments and in front of libraries (Why is this? Shouldn't they be *smarter* than that?), kind of akin to Victorian bedding schemes. Or bad white plastic hanging baskets dangling from porch perimeters, filled with tumbles of too-colorful petunias. I'm sure you're getting the picture. Needless to say, annuals are not a huge part of our lexicon. That is not to say, however, that we eschew annuals entirely. First of all, 95% of vegetables are stubbornly annual, and we are big on them. You might say immense. More on that in a subsequent chapter. Secondly, the Cutting Round is filled with decidedly annual cosmos, zinnias, and gomphrena, as well as the questionable dahlias, which we prefer to think of as perennials that need to be lifted and reinterred annually. We also employ annuals in very early spring, when there is very little on the immediate horizon, in several container plantings that cry out for embellishment, including a large basketweave pot at the center of the Cutting Round. For

To us, this combination of coleus and petunias has crossed the Great Divide to too much fun in a planting bed.

years, we filled these containers with pale blue pansies that so winningly complement the basic nascent green and white of that season; this spring, we switched it up, using instead an incredibly organic-feeling 'Picasso in Blue' miniature petunia, with a green flange around each of its soft purple petals. Our point is this: annuals definitely have their place, but don't let their instant chroma, which can easily veer into the realm of the overly extroverted, blind you to the fact that that they need to be thoroughly vetted by the aesthetic patrol.

central focus of the upper terrace. For instance, we have 8-foot-tall lollipop standards trained from solanum and solandra cuttings, equally impressive clipped-bay triple balls, and frame- and teepee-grown stephanotis, mandevilla, and jasmine, as well as a huge assortment of specimen begonias.

Begonias are one of our specialties at the nursery—we probably propagate and grow as many as 30 different varieties. And what about the family of rare 'Sir John Thouron' yellow clivias, divided from a single plant purchased at Longwood's Rare Plant Auction 20 years ago? Interesting and unusual plants are our passion, wherever they come from, whatever their habit or cultural requirements or preferred habitat, and we urge our visitors to contemplate the value of houseplants, which are thrilled to be outside in summer, as well as exotic garden plants to greenly enrich their lives, as the tropical palette offers so much delight and surprise (think echeverias, succulents, cacti, agaves, bromeliads, furcraeas, etc.). In the end, we want to expose our visitors to as broad a spectrum of horticultural possibility as is possible. That is what we've done for ourselves, and that's what we strive to do for those who come to tour.

Here's where we invite our visitors to enjoy their boxed lunches in season but, even in winter, the Terrace Garden maintains its architectural integrity.

 The artful use of hedging allows one to achieve garden "rooms"
of many different conceits and personalities, these at the Vrtba
Garden in Prague.

The Great
UNITERS

It is now the late 19th/early 20th century, and we must turn, again, in thanks to horticulturist William Robinson, whose Gravetye Manor in Sussex is one of the most enduring examples of classic garden design, and his devoted ally Gertrude Jekyll, who rescued garden design from a nearly catastrophic fall from grace. Robinson and Jekyll, as it transpired, not only sent Victorian bedding schemes packing, they were ultimately the great uniters, finally marrying the formality of the classical parterred and terraced school of thought with the picturesque school, and the result is what we now know as classic garden principles. The formula remains pretty much as they developed it, with garden "moments" becoming increasingly informal as one moves away from the house. Therefore, surrounding the house and mirroring its architecture to some extent might be a series of rooms hedged in box or hornbeam or yew, with "doorways" carved into the hedges so as to interlink the rooms. In one might be a classic parterre arrangement. In another, a rose garden. In another, color-themed borders surrounding a central piece of statuary. And in another, a substantial basin and fountain flanked by orange trees in Versailles boxes. Or perhaps the gardens fall from the back of the house in broad, balustraded terraces linked by stairways and ranks of pleached hornbeam or wisteria tunnels, with a great central water feature flanked by parterre beds on the highest level, borders flanking a central greensward on the next, with a formal orchard on the lowest terrace, this bordered at the far edge by a ha-ha, the whole then giving onto Brownian parkland and landscape. The key was effortless transitions that led seamlessly from one idea to the next.

DO

Identify both a plant and color palette in every sector of your garden, and stick with the plan. This is the fun of strolling a garden: that one wanders from one idea to another in a lovely succession of reveal and surprise. A garden that is planted in a single note has nowhere to go: you drink it in in a single glance and your experience is over. On any size property, it is far better to plan a progression of garden moments, each one different from the next and revealed teasingly through use of axis, enclosure, hedging, etc.

Consider the virtues of a small orchard. This can happen on any size property and can amount to as little as six semi-dwarf apples planted in a grid on a patch of lawn or meadow. There is something both classically conceived and infinitely homey about an orchard organized on a grid. Factor in that riot of blossoms in spring and the edible glory of fruit in the fall, and, truly, who couldn't use some?

Visit your local nurseries annually, and sign up for catalogs from non-local sources. This is the most fun any gardener will ever have: to discover something newly minted through hybridization and unlike anything that has come before. We just adopted two new kids on the block, *Styrax japonicus* 'Frosted Emerald' and *Davidia involucrata* 'Lady Sunshine' (with yellow-margined leaves), from our favorite variegated plant nursery, Broken Arrow in Hamden, Connecticut, and couldn't be more excited.

Strive for perennial plantings in every instance possible. We have nothing against annuals—save for the fact that they are stubbornly annual and need to be replanted every year. The wonder of perennials is that they will return every year and, usually, with more vigor than the year before. Will there be some attrition and failure? Of course. But, mainly, if you choose them correctly according to siting, they will faithfully reward you year after year.

Try a bit of clipped box or yew or hornbeam where appropriate on your property. Nothing so subtly crisps up a garden without adding an alternate hardscape texture than any of those manicured into a sharp-edged or mounded hedge or parterre enclosure. Additionally, many varieties of box will naturally form a globular or sentinel-like silhouette as they grow, and their addition to a garden can provide a very handsome architectural counterpoint to surrounding plantings: for instance, the balls of variegated box lining the Pine & Dogwood Allée and decorating the beds in the Kitchen Garden.

DON'T

Think of your plantings as a box of Crayolas spilled higgledy-piggledy in your beds and borders. All right: this is a reiteration of a prior caution but, honestly, using every color of the rainbow may be fine of a kindergarten morning but is not so when it comes to devising a color scheme for a garden. Start with a limited palette—you can always add to it over time if it's just too snoozy. To us, the most beautiful gardens offer up their wares with a delicious subtlety that is calming and thrilling in equal measure.

Concentrate solely on blossom color. With a very few exceptions, blossom is fleeting, but foliage, at least in season for the deciduous types, is forever; not only that, but so many cultivars will romance you with a dramatic change of leaf hue come fall. Foliage color can range from nearly true blue to chartreuse and deep burgundy, not to mention the many striking variegations, stripings, dapplings, and marginations available. And what of the reds, bronzes, and golds come autumn? Just think about it.

Ignore the gift of self-seeders. While not appropriate for severely regimented (à la the Dutch) or minimalist effects, self-seeders can create a spontaneity and wonderfully impressionistic effect that will add some becoming romance to almost any garden moment. Poppies, foxgloves, eryngium, fennel, feverfew, and forget-me-nots are just some of the perennial plants that are happy to procreate via seed. And keep in mind they can always be edited a bit or dug up and resited for your yearned-for effect.

Underestimate the virtues of groundcovers in locations that are simply too shady to support lawn. Yes, of course, there are hostas to enliven said precincts. But so will pachysandras and ivies, these both available in a range of colors and variegations and wearing, as the Finck's overall ads styled it, "like a pigs nose" ("The Man Who Thinks, Invests In Finck's"). And what about ajuga with its pretty purple wands in spring? Or vinca with its blue blossoms? Or creeping raspberry with its leathery leaves turning brilliant red in fall? Fail to investigate at your own peril.

Hesitate to mix your plants, à la a classic English mixed border, especially in your peripheral plantings. The classic scheme calls for smallish trees at the back, shrubs and the tallest perennials in the middle, and lower-growing perennials or groundcovers in the front row. This is an excellent solution when screening is an issue, particularly on typical suburban lots where your neighbors are a mite too close on either side, as it creates a dense yet truly decorative barrier.

8

Themed *Gardens*

The Cutting Round and French Garden are like a couple of horticultural polka dots cast on the hillside above the house.

As we have indicated (probably to the point of tiresomeness), horticulturally, we have been fairly adamant about the "farm appropriate" idea and respecting our very particular history, situation, and vernacular. However, that doesn't mean we are averse to culturally thematic or color palette ideas or a healthy dose of whimsy, which, to some, might border on the inappropriate, as many of our gardens are surprising not only for the unexpectedness of their siting but more than a few for the unexpected nature of their content as well. But, still, this is all in the tradition of the classical lexicon: borrowing elements like water cascades, pleached hedging, or ranks of pencil cypress from this culture or that (even replicating an indigenous style of gardening altogether),

or keying a garden to a limited palette or certain blossom color,
the ultimate being the white (or moon) garden, where only white
flowers are allowed, most vividly perfected at Sissinghurst in England,
that magical brainchild of Vita Sackville-West and Harold Nicolson.

   And what about all those surprising grottoes that proliferated
across Europe like wayward spawn after the gardening gene really
kicked in: marvelous stone-and-shell-work Bat Caves concealed in a
hill or such, with some surprising interior water feature? The floating
golden crown at Arundel Castle, again in England, which dances on
a spout of water inside the cloistered confines of the most elaborate
tile-and-shell-work dome, designed by Julian and Isabel Bannerman,
is surely a winning example. But Italy. England. France. America.
Name your grotto. And then there's the stumpery, one of the most
eccentric horticultural conceits ever hatched, involving a piling up of

tree stumps and roots, which are then planted with ferns and mosses, the prime example of this Victorian concept residing at Highgrove Royal Gardens in England. Or what about those gardens that have hijacked an ethnic style wholesale? There are Japanese gardens throughout the United States, including the Shofuso in Philadelphia and the Morakami in Delray Beach, Florida. If your climate will stand it, why *shouldn't* you have an English stumpery on the shores of Lake Michigan or an Italianate garden in Shanghai? The world, as they say, is your oyster!

The French Garden

Surely, there could be nothing more surprising than chancing upon a replica of the Eiffel Tower on a hillside in rural Pennsylvania. All we can say is that when you've spent your early life creating fantasy events like Renny did, sometimes you just have to roll with it. In fact, that very miniature of the Eiffel Tower (which, oddly, we purchased in Burford in the English Cotswolds) was the central feature at the annual April in Paris Ball in Manhattan for a good number of years until we finally retired it, having witnessed far too much diamond-adorned frivolity, to the farm. And, again in our defense, we would hazard to suggest we have managed to integrate such formal-verging-on-unconventional ideas into our rural landscape by siting them and surrounding them with sufficient informality. Certainly, the French Garden is our most formal statement on the farm with its parterre scheme of box-edged beds filled with purple ajuga and moss phlox, the four outer ones containing topiaried standard 'Miss Kim' Korean lilacs underplanted with catmint, with the miniature Eiffel Tower arising at the center from an *étoile* ("star") of four types of box: 'Variegata', 'Green Pillow', 'Little Missy', and 'Justin Brouwers'.

This circular garden "room" is entirely surrounded by "walls" of alternating rose hoops, snowball viburnums, and courses of 'Incrediball' hydrangeas. There are six rose hoops in all: we think the iron flourishes at the top of each must have been part of an antique grape arbor originally, but we have elevated each on a pair

The French Garden is certainly our most formal statement on the farm, but it is achieved so informally, we think it suits us.

of tall, stout, square, pressure-treated columns, each leg of each "hoop" boasting a pink or peach-colored climbing rose. Each hoop is then flanked by a pair of the now-stately snowball viburnums we bought at an end-of-season plant sale 30 years ago, and the courses of Incrediballs link viburnum to viburnum, so one may only enter into the garden through a rose hoop. The lilacs and viburnums, with their massive hydrangea-like blooms, flower in spring, followed by the roses in midsummer; the season ends with the hydrangeas and the sweet autumn clematis on the Eiffel Tower coming into blossom. Quite formal but, still, one generally encounters this garden totally informally, as a surprise as one achieves the summit of the slope coming up from the Dell, or as a random moment plopped on the green hillside to the west of the Kitchen Garden. And looking out from the center of the garden to the surrounding woodland, the aviary, the Cutting Round, the Kitchen Garden, and down toward the house across the drive, one definitely feels one is linked to the greater whole in a most intimate way.

Six rose hoops that ring the French Garden are each planted with a different pink or peach climbing rose.

OPPOSITE *From the French Garden, one can look out on the aviary, Kitchen Garden, Cutting Round, and down to the house scant yards away.*

The Mediterranean Garden

The Mediterranean Garden, centered on the village fountain, is planted with variegated agaves and willow-leaved pears masquerading as olive trees.

We presented displays at the Philadelphia Flower Show eight times in the 1980s and '90s, and while this involved a considerable amount of work (especially with regard to the growing on of plant matter for a horticultural show that occurs around the deeply frigid Ides of March), one of the pluses was the generous stipend one received to implement one's design. We had done installations ranging from a

Mughal garden to a French parterre scheme, and one year, decided
to create a truly classically themed idea. We were touring in France
the summer before and came upon a wonderful architectural and
garden salvage yard near Versailles that sold everything from parquet
de Versailles to ancient wellheads and fountains, stone coping and
balustrades, and small stone structures. It was there we discovered
both the village fountain that is the focal point of the Mediterranean
Garden and the gloriette that now graces the pool plateau. That year
in Philadelphia, the village fountain danced inside the gloriette in
our installation at the show, and then both were retired to the farm.

*As one wanders
down through the
Lajeski Meadow, the
Mediterranean Garden
is a near total surprise
as one encounters
the breach on the east
side of the garden.*

We knew the gloriette would provide a welcome bit of shade near the pool, but the village fountain was up for grabs. We had recently assumed that final 30 acres above and beyond the pool with our friend Glen's help, and so the idea of the Mediterranean Garden was hatched.

We have always been huge admirers of British garden designer Beth Chatto, whose gardens at Elmstead Market in England continue to be a mecca for serious gardeners and who championed and wrote enviable books on both dry and wet gardening. As the spot we had chosen for this idea lay naked to the sun in the middle of an upper pasture, Renny's vision was that our Mediterranean Garden, another circular affair centered on the village fountain, would be an ode to Beth and her theories on dry gardening, which, in effect, called for sustainable plants popping up through a bed of gravel. The Mediterranean Garden would, also, nearly be a secret garden, as it is almost entirely enclosed in a ring of pink-blossomed 'Nana Variegata' weigelas so, if one chances upon it as one wanders down through the Lajeski Meadow in spring, it is simply a big pink mystery until one enters it through a breach in the hedge.

The more formal access to it would be by a wandering turf lane trailing up into the Lajeski Meadow northeast of the Temple Canum, flanked by goldenrain trees and standard rose of Sharon, a purple barberry hedge at the back, and a border of catmint at the front. One is first teased by the sight of the village fountain up ahead and then, as one enters that enclosed space and it expands, one begins to understand the plantings that surround it. Sprouting through the gravel are a variety of grasses, sedums, euphorbias, variegated agaves, and even such exotics as hardy opuntias. And, flanking the fountain, a pair of non-bearing, willow-leaved pears looking for all the world like olive trees. We bring out pots of tropicals like agaves and furcraeas to enhance the Mediterranean mood in summer, and a whimsical driftwood bench offers the weary traveler a place to rest for a moment. Because of its near enclosure by the weigela hedge, one is truly transported to a place and vernacular awfully far away from a rural Pennsylvania hillside.

CLOCKWISE FROM TOP LEFT *Visitors are convinced we can grow olive trees in our zone 6b—until we tell them that these doppelgängers are really non-bearing willow-leaved pears.*

'Alumigold' scarab cypress, one of the many horticultural denizens popping through the gravel in the Mediterranean Garden.

A pretty indigofera and purple-leaved 'Diabolo' ninebark are among the floral delights of the Mediterranean Garden.

The Cutting Round

The Cutting Round is another circular garden about 18 feet in diameter, surrounded by a low clipped hedge of 'Gold Queen' euonymus and divided pie-like into eight segments by stone paths, with an antique basketweave stone pot and globular wire topiary form as the central feature. We include it in the themed garden chapter because it's planted exclusively with annual cutting flowers. Our usual mix in the parti-colored wedges is zinnias, dahlias (we know: call them what you will), cosmos, and gomphrena. This past year, we planted the massive central pot with 'Picasso in Blue' miniature petunia and a lavender-hued clematis to climb the topiary form. We sited this garden so that it is the visual destination at the top of the westernmost set of steps leading up from the drive and, also, the entirely symmetrical focal point out the west gate of the Kitchen Garden. It is right on the verge of the too colorful but, in a way, that is its point. It's a tiny, multicolored, confetti-flying garden party, contributing soon enough to colorful midsummer mixed bouquets,

The antique basketweave pot at the center of the Cutting Round holds a globular topiary form, this year planted with sweet autumn clematis.

OPPOSITE *We plant the Cutting Round exclusively with parti-colored annuals for cutting, usually zinnias, gomphrena, dahlias, and cosmos.*

This early spring shot of the Cutting Round, house, and Kitchen Garden fence, and their box and euonymus embellishments, shows the importance of architecture, hardscape, and green architecture in organizing a garden.

USE WITH CAUTION

This is going to be another slightly tiresome lecture on the merits and pitfalls of devoting yourself to a theme, or even several themes, in your garden. First of all, unless you just go whole hog toward a single, all-encompassing idea, like turning your garden into a miniature of Hidcote or Tivoli or Katsura or Versailles, themes, in order to amalgamate them into a greater whole, take room. However, if you really do want an English or Italianate or Japanese or French garden, and your site and zone will sustain it (or, at least, allow you to replace the ungrowable with the possible, as we have done, for instance, with the willow-leaved pears masquerading as olive trees in the Mediterranean Garden), we say why not? Do your research, condense the concept (keeping in mind spatial relationship and scale), and proceed. On a typical suburban lot, if you want England, a pair of terraced parterres leading down to borders with a focal feature at the end could be the ticket. If you want France, ranks of parterres, important hardscape, potted trees in Versailles boxes, and a fountain might be of the essence. For Italy, head toward pencil cypress, a water rill or cascade, and a grotto or small temple as a visual destination. For Japan, a naturalistic pond, bonsaied and clipped trees and shrubs, stands of grasses and bamboo, raked sand or gravel, and a teahouse will take you there. Just make sure not to overpopulate the

✢ *While we feature a number of "themed" horticultural ideas on the farm, we have been very careful not to turn it into a "theme park."*

idea. Pare it down and give it space, or you risk moving your aesthetic dial from theme to theme park. Be forewarned: this is a slippery slope. In terms of incorporating an idea like a moon garden or an Italianate or French pastiche into a greater garden scheme, the key here will be isolating the idea sufficiently through the use of screening, hedging, etc., so that it becomes this wonderful, magical surprise as one enters into it and then transitions subtly back into the greater garden.

in vases at any number of locations in the house. Vivacious, yes, yet not out of place because, if you look at that particular hillside in a casual northwesterly direction, what you see is a trio of polka dots consisting of the Cutting Round, the aviary, and the French Garden randomly cast upon a grassy hillside. Order and unpredictability. Structure and ease. Rural Pennsylvania meets a garden.

The Cutting Round is the visual destination at the top of the westernmost set of steps from the drive and the focal point out the west gate of the Kitchen Garden.

✠   *The White Garden at Sissinghurst in Kent is a simply gorgeous example
of exuberant cottage style as well as a single-color themed idea.*

Cottage
CHARM

One of Gertrude Jekyll's most important contributions to the ultimate union of the formal and informal was the introduction to the greater scheme of a small but very important sidebar in the history of the English garden, the cottage garden. Cottage gardening, as the name suggests, evolved from the types of gardens historically surrounding the least significant but perhaps most charming of all British architecture. Driving through British villages and countrysides, who hasn't been enchanted by those timbered and thatched tweenesses, their riotous patches of flowering shrubs and perennials managing to appear both spontaneous and exceedingly well tended? These relatively tiny plots were and are both utilitarian and lovely, edible and herbal plants commingling with purely decorative ones in loosely orchestrated beds, with some vague thought given to color and height; a course of box edging or some clipped yews, or a greensward or topiaried specimen or orchard, adds just the right amount of green gravitas to counterbalance the garden's seemingly artless profusion. Another feature of the cottage garden is its welcoming attitude to self-seeders, fall where they may, with an editing hand as only a last resort. As well, one will happily chance upon bits of organizational hardscape: a set of steps, a stone rim to a terrace, a ruined wall, as well as a handsome piece of statuary or charming water feature in these diminutive schemes. And, much like their classical counterparts, these may also transition seamlessly into a borrowed view of meadow or woodland or, most devoutly to be wished, the spire of the 15th-century village church glimpsed across a hedgerow.

DO

Do your research. If you want to emulate a particular garden style, make sure you are well acquainted with its specifics. What are the necessary hardscape underpinnings of this particular vernacular? Terraces? Colonnades? Ruins? Water features? What plants, including trees and shrubs, do these gardens generally contain? What are the closest cultivars of these suitable to your zone and site? The more you know, the more successful you will be.

Visit gardens related to the scheme you are envisioning. We suppose if what you fancy is, say, an Italian idea, you must have experienced a number of these to be so enamored. Return to them with a pad and pencil, make some drawings, take notes. Photograph the elements that intrigue you. Then return home and make a plan to scale. Let us reemphasize here the "to scale" idea: classic golden architectural formulas (height of step to riser, height to width, etc.) are there for a reason.

Feel free to extract lessons and elements from various ethnic vernaculars and combine them into your own unique garden vision. There's no reason your garden can't borrow from a number of cultures and be truly transcontinental in aspect. This does not mean, however, that you are at liberty to populate your Japanese teahouse with a family of German garden gnomes hung with Tibetan prayer flags. Let subtlety and restraint be your constant companions.

Have a rose garden, if you can: it is a theme that can work on many properties. Basically, this is a symmetrical parterre idea, in many cases foursquare with a central feature, the beds planted with a variety of shrub roses with perhaps a substantial central tuteur featuring a climbing rose as architectural ballast. We've also always loved the idea of columns linked by swags of thick roping at the back of a border with roses trained to climb the columns and follow the swags. Do pick a limited or at least complementary blossom palette, however, to avoid the Disney-esque.

Cleverly position a mirror or pair of mirrors on a wall, whatever your theme, but especially if your garden is small. Much like a piece of open water, they not only add sparkle and lightness and a material juxtaposition to green matter, they also enlarge the space by reflecting it back on itself. We've seen them used very successfully, for instance, as a circular faux oculus and visual destination in an ivy-clad wall at the end of a view or, equally, in pairs on a wall flanking a central feature. The key is the organic frame that will mask the edges.

DON'T

Underestimate the possibilities of a bog or water garden theme if you've got a pond or creek on your property. Edging such a feature with plants that love wet feet can not only help keep your banks from eroding but provide you with a garden moment that is unlike any other. Willows, cattails, grasses, irises, and water lilies are some obvious choices. But what about variegated sweet flag with its sunnily striped blades, or pickerel with its pretty pastel spikes, or the pencil-like silhouette of horsetail? Or, if you have a gently running stream, how about planting some lavish stands of watercress, one of the healthiest and most delicious greens on God's green earth?

Make the mistake of creating a cheap facsimile of your aspired-to vision. What you love about the theme you have chosen is most probably its age, the antique perfection with which it was executed, and the unimpeachable quality of the materials employed to create it. For instance, don't substitute cast concrete for marble or coral stone when it comes to stairways and balustrades. If classical statuary or a fountain is required, try to find one with some genuine age and patina. If potted specimens are part of your theme, put them in real terracotta, not faux. Quality is quality.

Overlook your own vernacular as being your potential "theme." Clearly, ours has generally been the "farmness" of things. However, if you are in a newly built home on a suburban lot, there may not be a whole lot with which to work. On such properties, we always think the smart thing to do is to "cottage" it up through the addition of porches, arbors, appropriate fencing, ornamental trellising, etc. The addition of a flag patio as an outdoor room out the backdoor—populated with comfortable furniture and some green enclosure, perhaps even a wisteria-clad arbor overhead—is an idea that seems applicable to a good many architectural vernaculars.

Ignore, if you're handy with a hedge trimmer, the possibilities of employing it to create topiary punctuation marks or even an entire topiary garden from box or yew in a part of your precincts. Consider the stunning lawn of topiaried box chess pieces at Haseley Court in Oxfordshire, England, or the sublime yew hedge carved into swans riding cresting waves at the Ladew Topiary Gardens in Monkton, Maryland. They can add really stunning green architecture to any garden scheme and are a tremendous bang for the buck, while being fun to imagine and create in the bargain.

Forget the native inhabitants of your forests and fields. Honor them by creating a themed habitat that is creature-friendly, particularly to birds, bees, and butterflies. For instance, a meadow-y planting of milkweed, asters, echinaceas, and black-eyed Susans will be marvelously attractive to butterflies, particularly Monarchs as they make their annual migration. Or berry-bearing shrubs and trees like viburnums, dogwoods, elderberries, serviceberries, winterberries, and chokeberries will certainly attract all manner of songbirds to your precincts. Good for them, good for you!

9

Edible *Gardens*

While various bamboo constructs have featured in the Kitchen Garden historically, the now-permanent central feature is an apple arbor, four semi-dwarf apples grown on an iron frame, with a planter on a column beneath it.

The rise on the north side of the house is where a good deal of architectural and horticultural jockeying for position takes place. Architecturally, there are the aviary, corncrib, mother-in-law house (home to our longtime farm manager Bob and his wife, Rose), and chicken house. Horticulturally, there is the French Garden, Cutting Round, Kitchen Garden, Herb Gardens, Edible Rooms, and Fruit Border. In the main, one simply wanders across lawn to these various destinations so that, in a way, this idea was all about siting the gardens in sympathy with the existing architecture, so that there was some symmetry to the overall plan.

At the heart of the farm, designing the gardens was all about siting them sympathetically so that they respected and enhanced the existing architecture.

In the end, what has been most interesting is that, surprisingly, it is not the big gestures we have created—like the allées, which are, pro forma, really garden gestures of their own—that needed concentration but more the micro questions of how to link the gardens at the heart of the farm with the farm buildings, these representing a good half of the equation. And, in a lovely way, this has allowed us to pay homage to the real personality of the farm. Farmness. A classically conceived Kitchen Garden. Herb Gardens. The Fruit Border. And a rather eccentric assemblage we call the Edible Rooms. All these in close proximity to all that deeply American architecture as well as the stalls and paddocks for the horses, sheep, and goats, and a chicken house full of fowl, both domestic and exotic.

The Kitchen Garden

We opted for a traditional kitchen garden vernacular: a rectangular plot, approximately 30 feet by 50 feet, surrounded by an ornate Victorian-inspired white fence (to match the trim on our outbuildings) with four gates, one in the center of each side, pea gravel paths, a viewing pavilion raised on the north side containing two Adirondack chairs and capped with a martin house, and symmetrically yet decoratively disposed raised beds composed of two courses of pressure-treated 8 by 8s. The pressure-treated idea remains an item of some debate; let us just say that pressure-treated wood is

*The quite traditional
Kitchen Garden resides
on the slope above
the house, with the
Cutting Round and
aviary providing visual
destinations out the
western gate.*

no longer treated with arsenic as a preservative and its propensity
to contaminate is so low as to be virtually undetectable, but this is
a personal call entirely. The central feature is an arbor composed
of four semi-dwarf apples trained on an iron frame, this flanked by
two square beds, clocked to form symmetrical diamonds, raised four
courses high and boasting towering permanent tuteurs with fanciful
Art Deco topiary form flourishes.

Hard architecture is important in a vegetable garden for a
number of reasons. First of all, you're constantly disrupting the
stubbornly annual planting by harvesting it, leaving bare spots to be
replanted in your wake, so the more crispness and definition you can
lend to the garden, the better. Secondly, architecture in a potager is
not only beautiful but increases both your real estate and chances of
success immeasurably. Raised beds displayed with an eye to design
not only lift the garden work up toward you and neatly separate
planting bed from path, but they amend more easily, heat up faster
in spring, and drain better. Additionally, vegetables, aside from the
climbing varieties, are, mainly, resolutely low-growing things, so any

vertical structure you can add not only adds much-needed height and visual interest to the garden but gives you plenty of growing surface for viners, like tomatoes, pole beans, squash, and gourds, on a relatively small footprint.

Aside from the two permanent tuteurs, we annually construct any number of bamboo tuteurs and teepees and even small pavilions tall enough to walk under in the Kitchen Garden and Edible Rooms, as we rotate crops from garden to garden. We've also taken to dividing the essentially large rectangular beds into smaller symmetrical increments by cleating in stout bamboo canes across the surface of the beds, which adds a very nice layer of organizational hardscape. And, finally, we've added four variegated box balls and an equal number of sentinel-like box topiaries to the center of some of the beds (symmetrically disposed, of course), and a pair of columnar apples flanking the steps to the viewing pavilion for even more

LEFT *We had to cut deeply into the north side of the Kitchen Garden to level it and, as a result, have long planting boxes and a viewing pavilion up several steps overlooking the garden.*

RIGHT *We favored a vaguely Victorian hardscape scheme here, capping the viewing pavilion with a tangle of trumpet vine and a substantial martin house.*

all-season interest. It's surprising how small gestures like these can have such huge organizational impact!

We then plant away with the most interesting vegetable varieties we can find, always with an eye to form and color as well as taste. The blue of brassicas and leeks and kale, the multicolored ribs of chard, tomatoes running the gamut from tiny Sungolds and Mr. Stripeys to the deep purple of the Black Russians to mammoth Great Whites and bicolored Hillbillys, the fantastic forms and colors of lettuces from deep crimson to nearly chartreuse with all kinds of splotches and dapplings, the surreal length of Chinese long beans: all contributing as rich a variety of color and form to the garden as any blossom could hope. The fun here is juxtaposition of form and color, just as you would consider in a flower border. There are, of course, also short- and long-season crops, and you'll want a mix of both. Some long-season stalwarts planted in spring that will continue producing until frost are kales, chards, leeks, eggplants (plant when soil has warmed up!), and onions. Cucumbers, squash,

The rule of thumb of raised beds is that they be shallow enough that their center is easily reached and no longer than is convenient to walk around.

OPPOSITE *Bamboo is our material of choice for the construction of auxiliary tuteurs and teepees, easily fabricated with a handsaw and a packet of zipties.*

cabbage, broccoli, and potatoes are also relatively long-season. Some short-season ideas are carrots, radishes, lettuces, and peas, these most successfully planted in early spring and again in late summer, and beans, which can be planted and replanted all season long. You'll want to keep track of what you plant where and when, as crop rotation is particularly important for solanums (tomatoes, potatoes, eggplants) and brassicas (cabbage, broccoli, Brussels sprouts) to avoid soil-borne viruses, this best done in at least a three-year cycle. Equally important is annual soil amendment with green, animal, or bagged manures. Pour it on, fork it through, rake, and you're ready. Honestly, there is truly nothing like vegetables freshly harvested from your own plot. If you have never grown your own, you really should.

The Herb Gardens

If one forges up that easternmost set of Philadelphia curbstone steps and the grassy slope it accesses, the most immediate visual destination, straight ahead, is an Atlas cedar and an antique dovecote with its resident doves. Behind that are twin herb parterres, an herbal knot garden, and the Edible Rooms, all on a direct axis with the top of the steps, with the chicken house directly to the right. Again, this was a matter of siting the gardens sympathetically with the existing architecture. In this case, much of the work was done for us, as the chicken house was originally a carriage house: a clapboard affair on a stone foundation with great doors on the southern front. We simply closed the doors, cut a little door in one of the big ones, and added further stone foundation and a penned-in run for the chickens with a wisteria arbor at the top. The bonus was that there was an identical stone foundation with exactly the same footprint directly to the west of the carriage house (probably another carriage house) but no building. Its elevated profile, when filled with well-draining sand and soil, made it the perfect spot for a Medieval-style herbal knot garden. So we accentuated the foundation walls with clipped box and punctuations of dwarf Alberta spruce and constructed low stone dividing walls, à la the Medieval idea, to provide planting pockets for

TOP LEFT *We lay bamboo canes across the surface of the big beds, so as to create smaller, more manageable planting pockets; they are easily removed for soil amendment.*

TOP CENTER *What is there to say about tomato time in the garden: so many wonderful shapes, sizes, and hues—and such incredible, only-in-season taste!*

CLOCKWISE FROM TOP RIGHT *Purple Vienna kohlrabi, Jersey Supreme asparagus (new crowns just going in), spring raab, One Ball summer squash, Indigo Rose cherry tomatoes, and MacDonald rhubarb are just some of the stunning varieties available to the curious kitchen gardener.*

a variety of culinary herbs, as well as a square stepping stone pathway halfway to the center, surrounding an 18th-century English sundial we had picked up in our travels. And, finally, we added two stone steps on axis with the top step from the drive to enter the garden from the south.

Another great Renny, Inc., bequest, which became an annual source of very specific plant material, were the dwarf Alberta spruces he sold potted and pre-decorated at his New York shop as apartment-sized Christmas trees. Any that hadn't sold made their way to the farm post-Christmas and were employed in a number of intriguing ways, most notably flanking those new sets of steps upslope from the drive and providing some green architecture for the Herb Gardens and warren of Edible Rooms. Essentially, we planted them in small groves and then, about ten years in, made the decision to limb them up by removing the lower two to three feet of their skirts so as to increase both sun penetration and planting space. Now, 40 years in, they have achieved the decidedly eccentric charm of little Hobbit forests. Thymes, oreganos, mints, and occasionally sages are winter

We constructed the herbal knot garden by the chicken house inside the stone foundation of an old outbuilding that had disappeared long before our arrival.

OPPOSITE *The focal point of the herbal knot garden is an 18th-century English sundial, here surrounded with garlic chives in bloom.*

Groves of dwarf Alberta spruce, a yearly bequest from Renny's New York shop post–Christmas, add all-season charm to the warren of herbal and edible gardens that surround the chicken house.

Together the Herb Gardens form a symmetrical architectural grid, the herb parterres purposefully mirroring the dimensions of the nearby chicken house as well as the herbal knot garden.

hardy where we are; substantial stands of rosemary and lemongrass we pot up and overwinter in the greenhouses; and, annually, we grow and add things like lemon verbena, chamomile, dill, cilantro, tarragon, and winter and summer savory, each little planting pocket large enough for six to twelve plants.

We then hit upon the notion of herb parterres to flank the grass path leading to the herbal knot garden steps and, together, exactly mirroring the footprints of the herbal knot garden, chicken house, and penned-in run so that, in essence, we've got four identical squares totally symmetrically disposed on a grassy hillside. The parterres we edged in box with box sentinels at the corners and swirling topiaries at the center of each. We then divided the interiors of the beds into four parts, each with more low stone walls, with perennial chives and blood-veined sorrel occupying two in each, the other four being given over to Thai, lemon, lime, and Genovese basil annually. So one ascends the steps from the drive, travels the turf lane described by the parterres up into the herbal knot garden, and, exiting the herbal knot garden on the north side through another opening, one then enters the Edible Rooms, with a central clipped poncirus tree as the final visual destination to that whole axis.

LEFT *Chives are a real gift to any edible garden: they're perennial, indispensable in the kitchen, produce a truly winning blossom, and, when cut back, will regrow with fervor.*

CENTER *The herb parterres are planted with perennial stands of chives and blood-veined sorrel, then annually with four types of basil, including Mrs. Burns' Lemon, showcased here.*

RIGHT *Thai basil not only has a distinctive spicy tang, its purple stalks and veins and heavenly-scented flowers are lovely enough to be included in a mixed bouquet.*

The Edible Rooms

We are the first to admit that the Edible Rooms were gardens in search of an identity for a good number of years and, unlike most of the gardens, were truly additive in nature. We began this journey because, due to the strictures of crop rotation and sun requirements, we needed to find new planting space for the tomatoes, so we established a pair of square garden "rooms," each with the same footprint as those in the Herb Gardens, one a step up from the other, on the slope behind the chicken house, adding still more linear symmetry to the whole arrangement. Each of these we divided into four beds with a small, central feature with cruciform paths, then surrounding the whole with trellised walls for the growing of vines

and, outside those, box hedges with punctuations of dwarf Alberta spruce. For the first few years, we erected various bamboo constructs in them to accommodate tomatoes, beans, or squash, but there was something naggingly incomplete about the vision. We then planted that poncirus tree, hoping that adding that visual destination out of the north end of the Herb Gardens would add a sense of completion. It didn't. That vacant grassy hillside was still crying out for further development.

Renny suggested we carve two courses of crescent-shaped island beds for the planting of wandering vegetables like squash or cucumbers or melons into the turf, semi-circling the poncirus, with their final downslope edges matching exactly those of the two "rooms" in a firm axis running east behind the chicken house. We

The poncirus, which we clearly keep clipped, is a hardy citrus notable for its tiny white blossoms in spring, tiny orange-like fruit in fall (edible but achingly tart), and genuinely lethal, inch-long thorns.

TOP LEFT *A tomato teepee inhabits a quadrant of one of the square rooms in back of the chicken house.*

TOP RIGHT *A late-summer harvest of Adirondack Blue and Yukon Gold potatoes, garlic, and Walla Walla sweet onions, fresh from the garden.*

CENTER *This past season, the outer crescent beds in the Edible Rooms were planted with teepees of Gita and Red Noodle Chinese long beans, with potted fig trees sunk in the middle beds.*

BOTTOM *We now grow the trellis walls with Issai hardy kiwi and magnolia vine, all parts of which are important ingredients in Chinese traditional medicine.*

OPPOSITE *This past season, we grew Adirondack Blue and Yukon Gold potatoes in the lower square and cucumbers and cucamelons on bamboo frames in the upper square.*

backed the outer crescents with the same arrangement of trellis walls and box hedging as we had with the two rooms and then hoped to stand back and view a garden with its integrity intact. We did not. It still wasn't cohesive. Finally, we ripped up the interior turf paths, lined all the beds with metal edging, installed large blocks of stone where paths ultimately met grassy hillside, and pea-graveled all the paths, as we had in the Kitchen Garden. And, finally, about ten years from original conception, we had a garden. We now grow the trellis walls with two perennials: Issai, a bite-sized, fuzzless hardy kiwi, and magnolia vine (*Schisandra chinensis*), whose fragrant white spring blossoms eventually transform into lovely red berries. This past year, the outer crescent beds were given over to tall bamboo tuteurs of Chinese long beans and a pair of venerable fig trees in pots, the inner beds to Walla Walla and Redwing onions, the upper square room to cucumbers and bite-sized Mexican sour gherkins (cucamelons), and the lower square to Adirondack Blue and Yukon Gold potatoes. It's all in the adventure, right?

The Fruit Border

We are really loath to write about this idea at present as, however bravely and optimistically it was conceived, we have dropped the ball on it in the past few years. A book on interesting fruit cultivars we produced inspired us to plant this border along one side of the old riding ring, where there already stood a considerable grove of elderberries. Part of the idea was to mask the view of the pool plateau from that vantage point, so that it was a total surprise as one looked down the Perennial Borders. To that end, we planted some small trees at the back of the border against the post and rail fence, including cornelian cherry, the lacily burgundy-leaved 'Eva' elderberry, 'Contorta' flowering quince, a medlar, and a few soon-to-be medium to large shrubs like currants, chokeberry, winterberry, goji berry, and honeyberry. At the front, we trialed cranberries, strawberries, and dwarf blueberries. We did next to nothing to amend the soil, figuring there must be a lot of old cow shit in the neighborhood and, to our additional discredit, bought probably-too-infant plants from a West Coast grower. We planted, watered, and, basically, expected it to flourish on its own. It did not. Some of the plantings worked for a while. Some expired immediately. Then, about four years ago, the entire stand of vintage elderberries expired and needed to be removed, basically denuding the most mature part of the border. At this point, we have a substantial barrier of trees and shrubs at the more cloistered south end of the border and a few specimens at the top, but the entire middle section needs to be reconceived. This is another "watch this space" idea, but rest assured: we're on it.

Sadly, what is left of the Fruit Border at the south end, near the upper barn: we promise to make this a priority next season.

One of the many bamboo constructs we've built over the years, this
a pavilion in the Edible Rooms for climbing beans.

BAMBOO STRUCTURE

If we had to pick a single material we could not garden without, it would have to be bamboo. In the nursery, we use it to support potted vining plants like jasmine, stephanotis, and mandevilla, and in the borders, to stake lilies and dahlias. Its most thrilling use, however, is the construction of teepees, tuteurs, and even small pavilions, these being not only strong and durable but immensely pleasing to the eye. The two basic forms we employ in the Kitchen Garden are the classic teepee and obelisk. All you will need to accomplish these are a bundle of 8-foot canes, a bundle of 8-inch zipties, a small handsaw, and a wire nipper. To construct a teepee, stab six canes, fat end first, into the ground equidistantly and as deeply as possible in a circle about 30 inches in diameter. Gather the canes together centrally at the top and secure them firmly with a ziptie. Bingo! Done! The obelisk shape takes a bit more work but is more refined and infinitely more adaptable. To construct one for, say, climbing beans, you will need to use your handsaw to supply yourself with four 6-foot lengths and eight 2-foot lengths. Stab the four 6-foot lengths into the ground to create a 20-inch square. Then take four of your 2-foot lengths and eight zipties and connect the tops of the vertical canes neighbor to neighbor, overlapping them with the cross pieces by 2 inches at each corner. Tighten the zipties as firmly as possible. Then take the other four 2-foot lengths and attach one firmly to each corner with another ziptie so that it projects upward. Finally, gather the ends of those four canes at the top and secure them centrally with a last ziptie. Use your wire nippers to cut the tails off of the zipties to neaten and you're done. You can create a like structure on a bigger footprint for, say, tomatoes, by enlarging the square to 44 inches, employing eight 6-foot canes, four in the corners and four in the middle of each side, then binding them with 4-foot canes squarely at the top and using 3-foot canes at the corners to make the peak. For added strength, we often cross brace each side on these larger structures by stabbing additional 6-foot canes diagonally in an X on each side, each cane extending from every bottom corner to be firmly ziptied near the top of the neighboring vertical. Ziptie where the Xs cross as well. When firmly built, these constructs can last a good five years.

 Azaleas were just one of the foreign introductions that dramatically altered the face of both Continental and American gardens, these at Winterthur in Delaware.

Wild Ideas

To the admirable marriage of informality with just the right dash of formality that so defines classical garden theory, William Robinson, above all, championed a complete renunciation of artificiality in any form and a return to nature in its most refined persona. He was adamantly against any plant tortured into an unnatural shape, like topiaried box and yew, or roses and other shrubs and vines grafted or clipped into standards. He eschewed statuary and overly elaborate hardscape and water features. He railed against anything sham, particularly any attempt to replicate foreign vernaculars like Japanese or Italian gardens on native soil. His preference was, in general, for a replication of what Mother Nature did herself, adding only a deft managing hand and involving hardy perennials and native plants in great naturalistic drifts and intensive plantings of groundcovers and spring ephemerals that would positively carpet slopes and woodland understories. This, however, did not mean he chose to dismiss beds and borders, his brimming with choice plant matter, or prissily limit his plant palette to what was native to the British Isles. In fact, his most game-changing notion was the theory of "wild" planting. And far from championing a return to wilderness, he instead wrote, in and of *The Wild Garden* (1903), that "the idea of the wild garden is placing plants of other countries, as hardy as our hardiest wild flowers, in places where they will flourish without further care or cost." The introduction of plant matter from the Americas, greater Europe, and the Middle and Far East, from the potato and peach to kalmias and magnolias, had moved the Continental plant palette into wondrously unexpected territories. To these, Robinson now added oceans of Virginia bluebells, asters, and trilliums, alpine plants for rock gardens, and the rich colorations of newly introduced azaleas. Suddenly, the basic green of Kentian and Brownian parklands could be anointed with carefree color, elevating an already remarkable idea to an even greater luster.

DO

Raise your beds if you want to have a vegetable garden that's both beautiful and productive. Beds can be built out of a variety of materials from wood to brick, Belgian block, or stone. You can even purchase composite planks and corner constructs that allow you to simply slide the planks into the corners and secure them with screws. Do raise your beds at least 10 inches (more if possible) and, if you are using something as simple as 2 by 8 boards, on the longest sides be sure to stake them into the ground at the midpoint to avoid them bowing out over time.

Rabbit-proof your garden, or there will most certainly be tears before bedtime. Rabbits may hop but they essentially burrow, so this enterprise will entail renting a trencher and digging a 14-inch-deep trench under your fence line, lining it with stout iron grid, and stapling it to the bottom stretcher of your fence. If your fence has open pickets, line it entirely with chicken wire stapled to the top and bottom stretchers. Don't neglect your gates or the areas underneath them. Forewarned is forearmed.

Go online, Google "vegetable seeds," and order catalogs in the fall so you can spend the winter perusing and ordering from them. Some of our favorites are Johnny's Selected Seeds, Seed Savers Exchange, Vermont Bean Seed Company, John Scheepers Kitchen Garden Seeds, and Totally Tomatoes. You will find that you will have perennially favored varieties over time but, also, you're sure to discover a winning new cultivar each and every year. This is the fun!

Think about adding height to the garden through the use of vertical structure for climbing varieties of vegetables. As noted, this not only increases your gardening real estate on a relatively small footprint but also adds a healthy dash of enviable architecture. These constructs can embrace many personalities, from the very rustic to the very refined. Choose a material, be it bamboo, saplings, string trellises, or pre-constructed metal (the ones they sell for fancy rose tuteurs) that suits your vernacular and dispose them symmetrically in your garden as focal points.

Plant your garden with an eye to color and textural juxtaposition. For instance, pair Black Tuscan kale with a stout corn and Joseph's Coat amaranth. Or leeks with Australian Yellowleaf lettuce and Pink Lipstick chard. Or Giant Golden purslane with Bull's Blood beets and Savoy cabbage. The combinations are endless and endlessly exciting, and there's no reason your vegetable garden should be any less beautiful and chromatically managed than your most extravagant border.

DON'T

Put your vegetable garden too far away from your kitchen, otherwise, you will never get there often enough. The optimal siting for a vegetable garden is a flat area that gets at least six hours of full sun and, preferably, a whole day's worth. Square or rectangular are the obvious shapes, but a circular garden with pie-shaped beds and a central feature can also be of interest and, with the idea of raised beds, you could even construct a vegetable garden into a south-facing slope with your bed construct built into the slope to create flat, stepped surfaces.

Be dissuaded from the idea of a vegetable garden because your gardening space is limited. It's perfectly feasible to have containers of vegetables and herbs on your deck or patio. Get a couple of galvanized tubs or feed troughs, drill them for drainage, and have at it. Or line the perimeter of your deck with "window boxes" and plant away. Or, really, just an assemblage of terracotta pots is sufficient for herbs, lettuces, and some tomatoes (Tumbler, Patio, and Better Bush tomatoes are actually bred for container gardening).

Overlook the charm of having your very own asparagus patch. While it is, in effect, a one-trick pony and, even with one-year-old crowns, you will have to wait for the third year to harvest, once established, your asparagus bed will reward you with an admirable crop for up to 25 years. A perennial vegetable idea is a rare thing and, therefore, nothing to sneeze at, and the fronds left to grow will reward you with an additional show in fall when they turn an enchanting gold, with the female crowns displaying the added glamour of bright red berries.

Forget about your watering mechanism. This can range from a good old garden hose with a wand to pop-up sprinkler heads to drip irrigation. Drip irrigation is championed by many because it delivers water to the roots of the plants rather than their leaves and fruit. The downside is that it makes soil cultivation a trial with so many drip hoses running through the beds. We have opted for pop-up heads in the four corners of the main vegetable garden that spray toward the center as well as a hose and wand for spot watering.

Dismiss the attractions of edible flowers. We always plant a bunch of 'Alaska' heirloom nasturtiums, with their white-splotched leaves, to line the paths in the Edible Rooms and are very fond of Mexican mint, a far hardier substitute for French tarragon, as it has really lovely, tiny marigold-like yellow flowers. And, of course, runner beans have beautiful sweetpea-like blossoms, eggplants pretty purple ones, and okra, which is a member of the mallow family, has a truly stunning pale yellow, ruby-throated flower. Yet another good reason to plant a vegetable garden!

Forty years on
seems a good time
to reflect a bit. We
came to this place in
our young adulthood
with armloads
of aspirations, good
intentions,

We hope what sets Hortulus
Farm apart from other gardens
one can visit is that we are
more than a garden: we are an
entire experience that, hopefully,
connects our visitors with all
aspects of nature.

and vague dreams of carving out a place of solace and respite for ourselves. Chasing our Eden. And, placing one foot in front of the other, we surmounted the challenges, celebrated the successes, pushing ever outward from the heart to embrace every one of the farm's eccentricities and errant charms. We identified our essence, learned to bend the rules of classical horticulture to suit our uncooperative topography, and pushed boundaries to the extremes of American farmstead appropriateness. So, as we step through the doorway of advancing age, what on God's green earth have we wrought? Our intentions were to create a garden that respected our historic architecture and vernacular, followed the lay of our land, was inclusive of our many wooded and pastured areas, and allowed formal-esque statements to occur where both feasible and desirable. To date, we have established almost two dozen garden "moments" on 30 of our 100 rural Pennsylvania acres. Our hope was that they would be like little pops of horticultural surprise in what, in the

grand scheme, would appear to be a fairly artless and pastoral rural landscape. In reality, though, had we created an assemblage of one-off "trees"—a regular arboretum—without giving sufficient thought to the greater "forest"?

Had we managed to achieve a sympathetically woven fabric, catching up the many colored strands we had chosen to employ, or some tasteless, supersized miniature golf course, lacking only a waterwheel and lighthouse to really put the icing on the cake? In the end, we knew we would only succeed in our vision if we could link our various "trees" into a unified forest with such subtlety, one would never be jarred but only surprised and delighted as one wandered the farm, with our choices appearing to be so naturally revealed, so intrinsic to their spots on earth, there would be no question that they were exactly what and where they should be. So our charge became—through the thoughtful use of hardscape and turf and bark and stone and gravel and lawns and lanes and stairways and bridges—to weave our various gardens into a piece of whole cloth.

And our journey to wholeness continues to this day, for there will always be something new to be learned, some innovative and exciting cultivar to be considered, some loss to be turned to fresh possibility, some unanticipated design idea that has taken the horticultural world by storm. And then the task becomes how to integrate it into an already mature garden scheme. But that's the thrill of gardening, isn't it, especially of a perennial nature? To chance upon

something new . . . an idea . . . a scheme . . . a stunning variety. And then to trial the recent introductions and plant a few—or perhaps a bunch—and watch them mature over a number of years until they are the ones leading the show. Surely, there needs to be some management of the native disorder of things but, in the main, short of a terrible, killing winter, the plants simply continue to regale you with about five times the oomph with which you originally planted them. And you just stand back and say: "Wow. Wow." As if you had absolutely nothing to do with their place in your world. How wonderful is that?

Sharing

When we started our garden making, the gardens were for us. They were the end-of-the-workweek panacea that would lift us up and away from the insistent trials and incessant tribulations that dog any urban worker faced with the kind of pace and rigors associated with the vocations we chose, particularly in Manhattan. Garden work was the exact opposite of that tightly wound, please-the-client, get-the-presentation-on-the-table kind of pressure under which we both worked. We traded jackets and ties for jeans and work gloves and had nothing in our ears but the sounds of nature. Our birds. Our dogs and cats and chickens and horses. And instead of conference room tables and deadlines and tension, we had the blissful solitude of working with Mother Nature and finding a considered, unhurried, optimal solution to the particular parcel of earth that currently occupied our attention. For one to whom an interest in gardening came late, you can't imagine how eye- and heart- and soul-opening this was. If you have never breathed in for three beats, held that breath for three beats, then slowly breathed out for three beats in the embrace of a natural space you have helped to create, filled with birdsong and the dancing of butterflies and your dogs sunning at your feet, you have never felt something essential. Connection. As primal as a scream or a laugh or an anxiety-reducing sigh to every living thing. And you can't imagine how wondrous that is.

We have incorporated places of repose and contemplation throughout the gardens: as with all gardeners, we should learn to use them more.

Being able to host community charity events around the pool—and we have had many—is one of our greatest pleasures.

We first started opening up the gardens to visitors about 25 years ago. A friend who was a member of a nearby garden club asked if she might bring her group for a visit. At that point, we had never really considered that anyone might be interested in visiting us. However, here's where we run into another inevitable and pretty much fundamental truth: all gardeners are pleased to show off what they have created, especially to those with a keen interest and similar horticultural knowledge. So, on a pretty morning in late May, 17 ladies from Princeton, New Jersey, in a variety of garden chapeaux with scarves daintily knotted about their brims, arrived at the nursery to see what we had wrought. We were thankful that most had opted for sensible walking shoes, as I don't think they really fully understood the journey that lay before them. One assumes they envisioned a pretty garden surrounding a home divided into the expected manicured rooms, the most challenging aspects of exploring them perhaps involving a few sets of garden steps.

By the time we had led them from the nursery parking area down the Birch Walk to the lake, most of them began to appreciate the particulars of what might lie ahead. This was not a gentle stroll through a condensed series of dulcet garden moments but more, in fact, in the line of a good trek through a sizeable park with plenty of ups and downs. By the time we had encircled the lake, climbed up into what was to become the Dell, then up to the French Garden, the Kitchen and Herb Gardens, down past the barns to the Perennial Borders, out to the Pool Garden, up the Pine & Dogwood Allée to the Urn Garden, down through the Lajeski Meadow to the Mediterranean Garden, then back down the Perennial Borders to a glass of lemonade and a gingersnap in the Terrace Garden below the house, there was a good deal of handkerchief dabbing, hat fanning, and catching of breath going on. And they still had that climactic climb back up the Birch Walk to the nursery to look forward to. As they finally collapsed into their cars, we were assured they had had a good time. Certainly, we hoped that was the case.

And, in that moment, our outlook shifted. The garden was, suddenly, no longer just for us. Our pleasure. Our green experimentation. Our private solace and satisfaction. And in truth, in our hearts, we knew this would inevitably be the case. Horticultural experimentation and education was always in the back of our minds as we created the gardens, even if the only students we enrolled were friends, the odd visitor, and ourselves. In the end, the gardens had become a series of progressive gestures that introduced anyone interested to new plants, fresh schemes, and novel ways of achieving a certain mood or resonance or cultural reference in our zone 6b. As well, particularly around the newly fashioned pool plateau, they provided a welcoming space for us to host events for the charities with which we continue to be involved, including the local SPCA, libraries, social services, and HIV/AIDS prevention and support organizations. We have tried to be good, caring constituents of our community and are sincerely elated to be able to show our support and give back in this way. But, mainly, our mission, slowly and inevitably, became the introduction of any aspiring gardener to a new world of possibility.

The Road to Publicness

One of our specialties at the nursery is topiaried, clipped, and frame-trained specimens like these hibiscus, lantanas, and oleanders.

Subsequently, the local historical society asked if we would open our garden for them on their annual fundraising garden tour day. We, of course, complied. Then more garden clubs began to inquire about visiting and, finally, a few more years in, we decided it might be wise to formalize the idea of visitation a bit. So we put some discreet numbers in the various gardens and had an illustrated map printed with numbers that corresponded to them and opened the gardens for self-touring on Wednesdays and Saturdays from May to October for a nominal fee. We then constructed some greenhouses up near Thompson Mill Road, turned the old farm shed into a nursery

office and visitors' entry, and opened Hortulus Farm Nursery, with the intention of propagating and offering for sale many of the hard-to-find plants featured in the gardens as well as interesting tropicals and, particularly, begonias that had caught our attention. Over time, we have also become known for the topiaried and frame- and cage-trained specimens we produce, a good number of these fairly unique in the trade. One handy offshoot of the idea of promoting tours of the garden was that every visitor would necessarily have to pass through the nursery where, hopefully, after finding inspiration in the gardens, they would be equally inspired to purchase a few of the plants with which they had become newly acquainted.

Were we overwhelmed with visitors? Not by a long shot. But word slowly spread, and every subsequent year would see a happy increase in numbers. We began offering guided tours by appointment

Our display greenhouses are full of interesting tropicals, most notably our large collection of unusual begonias.

to groups of eight or more as an increasing number of garden clubs made applications for visitation. Additionally, we had slowly been collecting vintage garden books, 18th-century Delaware Valley furniture, and Bucks County Impressionist paintings and ended up achieving quite notable collections of all these, with, for instance, over a thousand titles in our horticultural library. So we began to offer a "museum" tour, in which we would take groups through the collections housed in our lower barn library and the first floor of the Isaiah Warner house, as an add-on to a guided garden tour.

Then we got a call out of the blue from a now-defunct magazine called *Kitchen Gardener*, which was interested in doing an article on our vegetable plots. This, of course, was an immense validation for a gardener who was basically a horticultural neophyte before moving to the farm, and we're still unclear as to how they found us in the first place. Still, out they came and, in a few months, we were the proud recipients of our first magazine coverage. Further surprises ensued as, in the coming years, a good number of magazines and newspapers did articles on the farm and gardens. This, of course, begot more interest in visitation. We joined Greater Philadelphia

LEFT *One of our missions is to showcase new ways of growing, as in the bamboo frames in the Edible Rooms, which will keep these cucumbers both handsome and contained.*

RIGHT *"Where History and Horticulture Meet" has become our tagline for the farm, and we feel it sums up our intention very well.*

OPPOSITE *Now groups of eight or more can add a "museum" tour to their garden excursion to view our collections of garden books, Bucks County Impressionist paintings, and 18th-century Delaware Valley antiques.*

Gardens, the organization that celebrates "America's Garden Capital," with more than 30 public gardens, including such famed horticultural destinations as Winterthur, Longwood, and Chanticleer, within 30 miles of Philadelphia. Finally, in 2004, after 25 years of garden making, we made the decision to throw our lot in entirely with the farm. To that end, we sold our apartment and left our jobs in New York, moved full-time to Bucks County, and created the Hortulus Farm Foundation, a 501c3 not-for-profit foundation, whose mission is to leave Hortulus Farm as a fully public garden upon our demise.

We assembled an advisory board of wonderful friends and supporters, and crafted a mission statement, which pretty much sums up our feelings about the farm: "To inspire, educate, and delight. To represent and promote all that is best and most enduring about Bucks County by opening the gardens, house, museum, library, and collections to interested visitors. To establish Hortulus Farm as a permanent and important educational resource as well as a place of respite for individuals simply in need of reconnection with the natural world."

Recognition

Our growing reputation culminated in 2014 with Hortulus Farm being made an Affiliate Garden of the Garden Conservancy, an honor shared with only one other American garden, Jack Lenor Larsen's LongHouse Reserve on Long Island, New York. In 2017, *Garden Design* led off its "Great Gardens Across America" series with a feature on the farm, and *Flower* included us in its article "Must-See American Estate Gardens," in company with such august destinations as Old Westbury Gardens, Filoli, Middleton Place, and Vizcaya. We are now open most days of the week for self-touring between the first of May and the end of October and give "founder-guided" tours (yes, we are so old now, we have become "founders") to groups of eight or more (up to a busload of 50); we welcomed 5,000 visitors last year. This is thrilling and daunting in equal measure, but another extremely important lesson we have learned over time—an idea that has allowed us to take even deeper, calmer breaths when sharing our garden with visitors—is the plain fact that real gardeners are not interested in flawless perfection, they are interested in your reality. They want to know the full story, i.e., the reasoning behind the decisions and choices you have made that allow one to turn devastation or persistent concern into something pleasing and viable. Gardening is never about perfection: it's about process and adaptability and rolling with both the punches and the glorious successes.

So, when we give tours, we never shy away from the abundant issues inherent in having a 100-acre property being tended by a minimal crew of three or four. In fact, we engage our visitors in the process, encouraging them to ask questions and even supply answers. Do we have a drainage problem here? Indeed, as the muck sucks suggestively at their boots. Are our stately elms dying out? Yes. In fact that's one lying in massive chunks at your feet. Do we have to replace those 200 boxwoods after a winter from hell? Yes. We considered just spray-painting them green but decided against it. All this we follow by asking what their mitigating suggestions might be, and then we share our considered assessment and solutions, concluding with an exhortation for them to return five years hence to see how we did.

*Our gardens pay
courteous homage
to the beautiful
farm architecture we
inherited.*

Gardeners want to *share knowledge* above all else. Yes, on the whole, you want their takeaway to be: "I just saw the most amazing garden!" But, more, what you hope to inspire is: "I learned so much today." *And* was struck by beauty.

This last season, we received a lovely note from one of our visitors: "Maybe it was fall, maybe it was the perfect day, but your garden has catapulted itself to the top of my garden list. I keep trying to figure out why I liked the physical, visual, and sensual experience of being there over so many other gardens. Part is the loving attention you put into combinations of plants. Part is the formal design that merges into wildness in a gentle, natural way. Your birds and animals . . . Your garden feels natural and relaxed, making its visitors feel happy, at home, and relaxed, too. All in all, a perfect day." And close upon that receipt, another guest to the gardens sent us a poem she had written following her visit, which concludes, "today / there is no need to think / . . . let the spirit beauty drink."

The year is made of seasons but, to us, spring is the one that ultimately defines the gardener: we've certainly had a hand in creating its amazing spectacle, but to see the Woodland Walk suddenly be alive with the green of daffodils nosing their way up through a carpet of fallen leaves and the earliest magnolias opening their heavenly cups and the azalea buds just starting to show color— suddenly, the world is buzzing and life ignites. And then the show continues, with a little help, through spring and into summer, some garden characters fading, some coming on—a tapestry of plants and gardens and ideas that are, hopefully, woven into not only a satisfying whole but an emotionally rewarding experience. A stroll through nature that opens the eyes and warms the heart. That stops the stress of life for an instant and transports us to a place in which we truly feel at one with our planet and our earthly brethren: *our* place in the greater scheme of things. And, surely, this must be the definition of Eden. Not, of course, without its trials and tribulations, but these always balanced by the joy of triumphs and even unexpected glories. That first exultant spring when the newly planted redbuds bloom. A world on gorgeous fire as a ray of sunlight illuminates the autumn foliage of a tree. All we can say is, 40 years on, our garden has become its own creature and, while we continue to help it along, we are the constant recipients of such amazing surprises and rewards. "Let the spirit beauty drink."

If we may be so bold, *don't* hesitate: *do* imagine yourself a garden!

At this point, the gardens have really taken on a personality of their own that needs only a bit of management and maintenance to move into the future.

✟ *As shown in this shot of Great Dixter in Sussex, it is the
effortless transition from the formal to the informal that is
the hallmark of the classically conceived garden.*

Gardening 101

And so we circle back to what we've referred to throughout this book as classic garden principles, a striking amalgam of Italian, French, Dutch, and native British influences and, in the end, a scheme in which classically formal and informal styles coexist with ease. The key here was adequate formal garden structure counterbalancing a more informal parsing of the plantings, allowing one idea to progress in seamless stages to another. As well, by dividing the garden into a series of compartments or "rooms" through the use of screening, either by walls or hedging or terracing or the placement of stands of trees or massings of shrubbery, admirable gardens of a multitude of conceits, from mixed borders to bogs, allées, color-themed gardens, and orchards, could be created on nearly any size property.

In addition, the classical ideals of progression, reveal, axis, focal point, etc., were readily adaptable to any specific garden vernacular. And, perhaps best of all, armed with these classic notions, gardening became both comprehensible and available to anyone with an interest in it. Start with your home and its architectural style. Factor in your native topography. And, of course, identify your own unique vision of Pliny the Younger's *otium*—that very particular essence that will bring you the calm and serenity and sensation of oneness you so surely seek in a garden. And then apply the treasure trove of classic garden ideas to your garden, acknowledging the eccentricities and specificities of your site and bending the classic ideals to complement your own very specific "sense of place." You will never regret it.